Muhammad Al-Hallaaj

MORE THAN A DREAM

LIFE WITH JESUS CHRIST

salaam
MINISTRIES

Title: More Than a Dream, Life With Jesus Christ
Author: Muhammad Al-Hallaaj
Subject: Faith
muhammadalhallaaj@gmail.com

For more information or
additional copies of this book visit:
www.salaamministries.com

Available online at:
www.salaamministries.com/morethanadream

Printed and bound in Canada

Since ancient times no one has heard,

no ear has perceived,

no eye has seen any God besides you,

who acts on behalf of those who wait for him.

Isaiah 64:4 (NIV)

Preface

This little book briefly describes God's mysterious irresistible work in a man's heart. It is a love story – a story of God's amazing love for us.

A faithful young Iraqi Shiite tries to connect more closely with God through diligent duty. His search for God continues as he matures, his intellect doubting and disillusioned, full of questions for which he despairs of ever finding any answers. Finally he meets God in all his love, and finds he can trust Jesus even with his life.

> I sought the Lord, and afterward I knew He moved my soul to seek Him, seeking me. It was not I that found, O Savior true; No, I was found of Thee.[a]

It is not by accident or coincidence that you are holding this short account. The God who created the universe invites you to come into a relationship of love with him.

Read on....

---

[a] A Christian hymn. Author unknown

My Early Life as a Muslim

My name is Muhammad Al-Hallaaj. I was born in the Middle East in the city of Bagdad, the capital of Iraq. I was born into a Shiite [1] Muslim family.

When I was nine years old, we moved to the city of Al-Hella which is in the center of the district of Babel. It is about ninety kilometers south of Bagdad with Shiites as the majority group. I had many friends and neighbors there, most of whom were Shiite. I was brought up and thrived on the Shiite way of thinking and I was convinced it was the one and only way to Paradise. This was the sum of everything I knew to be true.

---

[1] It is well known that Islam is divided into two main sects: the Sunnis and the Shiites. The first group, the Sunnis, have four main orthodox schools. They are: The Malakite, the Hanfitic, the Shafiitic, and the Hanbalite. Each school applies the Sharia law exactly as it was passed down from certain important men who interpreted the most important doctrines. The schools neither develop nor change what they have been given. The other sect is Shiite. They always follow their "imam", the religious leader agreed upon by the world Shiite society. He has legislative power over them. All Shiites follow and apply everything he says.

I prayed three times daily.[2] I fasted during the month of Ramadan and made pilgrimages to Shiite holy places. I visited the grave of Imam Ali which is in the city of 'Annajif. He was the nephew of the prophet Muhammad and married his daughter Fatima. He is a holy man to Shiites who consider him "the door" through which one enters into Paradise. I also visited the graves of his sons, Imam Hussein and Imam Al-'Abbas, in the city of Karbala. I visited the graves of many other imams in Bagdad and Samara, all of them considered holy places by the Shiites. I would visit all the sites on a regular cycle.

In my heart of hearts I was pleading for the Day of Resurrection and forgiveness of all my sins. If these holy people were pleased with me and considered me good enough, God might allow me to enter Paradise where I would enjoy every kind of food and drink and seventy-two virgins, and live forever.

---

[2] Islam has five daily prayer times: 'alfajar, 'athuhur, 'al `asar, 'almagreb and 'al `asha'. The Sunnis pray all five times; but Shiites incorporate 'althuhur prayer with 'al`asar, and 'almagreb with 'al`asha, so that they pray only three times each day.

Like any good Shiite, I believed that the most important thing of all is to inherit heaven. Shiites obsess over it, always wondering how they can be certain of it. They believe that God is in heaven seated on his throne and on the Day of Resurrection he asks each person, "Are you Shiite?" If the person answers, "Yes", he goes to the right, to the side that leads to heaven. But if the person is from a different sect or religion then he goes to the left, to the side for those who are condemned, which leads to hell.

Because of this Shiites believe the right side is blessed and the left side is cursed. They forbid anyone to use the left hand to pass food since it isn't blessed. It is also the duty of Shiite men to let their beards grow without trimming them. Anyone who cuts his beard will not see God on the Day of Resurrection, which is why everyone must leave his beard long even when the temperature reaches 50°C (122°F) in the summer. We used to make fun of some of the young men who insulted God by not growing their beards, because God hated them.

We learned in the mosque that Sunnis have tails. We really believed it! The religious leaders also taught us that Christians have three gods and that they worship the Son of God. They taught us that Christians believe God was not alone but had a wife named Mary. She had a son named Isa. He was a Jewish prophet whom the Christians worshiped. We learned from the Quran that Isa was taken to heaven because he did not sin. The Jews tried to kill him, but God made someone else look like the Messiah. The Jews took him by mistake and crucified him thinking he was the Messiah while the real Messiah had already been taken up to heaven.

Before even mentioning the word "Jew" we had to say "God protect me from them". We believed that Jews and Christians would go to hell and that God would change them into the form of pigs. According to the tenets of Islam, Muslims are forbidden to eat pork. Since the Jews are the Muslims' worst enemies it is an obligation for Muslims to kill Jews – this is not forbidden in our law. Muslims believe a day is coming when they will make war on all their enemies, will kill all the Jews and all the earth will become Muslim. I didn't know why I had to hate the whole world, but I did! This is the religion I knew!

There were many things in our religion I didn't understand. An example is "temporary marriage" which the Shiites call "marriage of pleasure". It is a verbal agreement only between a man and woman. Witnesses or legal papers are not required. This marriage might last only one hour or one night or one month depending on the agreement. The sheikhs marry any girl they want in this way. But at the same time they would never let their daughters enter into this kind of marriage for pleasure! It is permissible for them, but not for others, because imams or sheikhs think they have a privileged position before God. For an ordinary Shiite, it would be impossible to ask them "Why?" because to even ask such a question could send you to hell!

In general, I wasn't the kind of person to ask a lot of questions in the mosque. I was an ideal, obedient, good Muslim. People saw me as an exemplary Shiite. They saw that everything I did was according to Sharia, but they couldn't see that on the inside I wasn't convinced of the things I was doing. Obedience was the only way I knew that could help me reach God and heaven where there were innumerable pleasures prepared and waiting for me. Iraqi people have suffered for a long time. Wars with our neighboring countries of Iran and Kuwait have created economic crises and food shortages over the years. My large family (we were eleven) suffered along with all the rest because we were poor and didn't have money to buy food. Despite all this suffering, we were comforted by the belief that in heaven everything we needed would be provided for free, everything we wanted – even seventy-two virgin wives. This hope gave us patience to endure our lives.

Muhammad Al-Hallaaj

I was obsessed with the question, "Am I going to heaven?" This and many other questions swirled in my mind at the time when I was just turning seventeen and entering my last year of high school (called "tawjihi"). Even though I was yearning to know the truth, I realized that the religious leaders did not have the answers to my questions. Where was I to turn?

Muhammad Al-Hallaj

My Journey Begins

One of our high school subjects was religion. Despite all my Islamic studies – at school or in the mosque – and despite keeping all my religious obligations to God, I had been unable to achieve any special relationship between God and me. I felt he was very far away from me, in the seventh heaven. I couldn't imagine it was possible that God would notice someone as insignificant as I was. I lacked inner peace and had no assurance that I would be going to heaven. I was constantly afraid.

We always used to look to Imam Ali bin Abi Talib, the cousin of the prophet Muhammad and husband of Muhammad's daughter, as the Caliph of God on earth whose teachings we should follow. And after this imam there was a chain of men beginning with the two sons of Imam Ali, al-Hasan and al-Hussein. This chain continued until the "waiting Mahdi" (called the "owner of time" by the Shiites). We glorified these men. With all these people coming between God and me, in my heart I realized I had no chance of entering the presence of God.

I began to think, in the end, that the reason I couldn't connect with God was because I was raised Shiite. So, after a long time of searching and discussing these things with my friends, I gave up trying to find God in Shiite Islam. I changed my sect and became Sunni. This caused a lot of trouble for me, especially with my family. My mother was particularly distressed. In her eyes I became an infidel by following the Sunni way. My family kicked me out of the house, so I went to live with some relatives. My search for God intensified. I began following Sunni practices, praying five times each day, not just three. For about two years I would study the Quran after the evening prayer.

I discovered there wasn't a big difference between the two sects. Sunnis glorify people just like the Shiites do. The Shiites glorify Imam Ali while the Sunnis glorify Omar bin Al-Khatab. When I studied Muslim books to try to find a route to God, I discovered there were different ideas in different books. This is when I began asking my questions aloud, but I couldn't find anyone with answers to the questions that troubled me. When I would ask someone he would abuse me, and accuse me of being a Zionist or a Jew or an infidel. I was afraid that if I kept asking I might get in trouble with the Imam, so I kept quiet and pretended I was convinced by their answers.

But I never found any Islamic sheikh who could answer my questions and I remained unable to connect with God.

I will give some examples of the type of questions I had. Maybe some of our Muslim brothers, whom we truly love, will read them and think about them. They may wonder if Islam is really the solution they think it is.

- Let's start with the Muslim holy book, the Quran. Muslims think there is only one Quran, the original of which is in heaven, and that it is infallible. But the real truth is that, until the third Caliph, Othman bin Afan, there were at least twenty copies of the Quran. There were many differences between these copies because each one contained different stories collected by different people. How did we end up with only one copy? Let me tell you what happened. When the Islamic army entered Azerbaijan from Arabia, the soldiers discovered that the northern Muslim army had copies of the Quran that were different from theirs. Each group claimed that their copy was the right one. Fights began to break out over the competing claims. Afraid the problems would escalate, the southern army leader, Hodhefa bin al-Yamaan, went to Caliph Othman bin Afan and explained the situation to him. The Caliph asked for all the copies of the Quran[3] to be collected.

Dear Muslim, can you remember how much conflict there was between Caliph Othman and some the other families due to his habit of choosing members of his own family to help him rule? Whenever they conquered a new city, he would assign members of his family to rule over it. That's why Abdullah bin Masoud (he was the best writer of his day and the best at memorizing the Quran) refused to relinquish his copy to the Caliph. At the same time, the Caliph refused to accept the copy Imam Ali bin Abitalab had in his possession because there was conflict between the al-Omuwiyeen and the al-Alaweyeen families.[4]

Othman collected what was agreed

[3]At that time the Quran was written on animal skins or tree leaves instead of paper, and some unwritten verses had been memorized.

[4]This is why the Shiites claim to have a special copy of the Quran called "Fatima's Quran".

to be correct, arranged it in order and divided it into small parts called "suras". (The word "sura" is Assyrian, not Arabic.) Each sura was given its own name. The whole Quran was called "Othman's Quran". All the copies of the Quran we have now are copies of Othman's Quran. It's possible, dear Muslim, to open the first page of the Quran and find this expression: "This Holy Quran is given to us by Othman bin Afan through the writer Hafs." This means that all the stories written in the Quran were told by Hafs and Othman agreed with him and began printing this book as an official holy book for Muslims.

And here we ask what does this expression mean? It means that the book we have is not necessarily God's word because many of the verses in the Quran are similar to the writings of various poets who lived before the Quran was compiled. You can survey three poets who lived before the advent of Islam: Priest Satiih, Priest az-Zabra and the poet Luis Sheikho. Examine their writings and those of their contemporaries. Their works are now forbidden in Islamic countries. If they are similar to the Quran, why are they forbidden? When I asked this at the mosque, they became very angry and they didn't settle down until I fled.

- Another of my questions had to do with the Quran and Sharia. The Quran is around six thousand verses. About seven hundred deal with law, worship, and relating to others. About two hundred verses are about personal laws, inheritance laws and civil laws. These two hundred verses are 3.3% of the total and some of them are not followed by anyone these days. The working law we use is less than 3% of the two hundred; to be accurate there are only eighty verses of the six thousand we actively work with. This reveals a weakness in the law. The question might arise, "Where do the leaders of Islam get all their laws and how do they apply them or judge by them?" Years later, I was to discover in further studies where most of Islamic Sharia law actually originates.

- Muslims claim that theirs is a merciful religion and that the prophet of Islam came with mercy for all people. Because of this, when I was searching Islamic history books to learn about God, I was shocked by some of the appalling stories I found. I don't want to relate all, or even some, of these

> stories; it's enough to tell you about one. It illustrates what will happen to the man who defies the ruler of a Muslim country. (In modern speech we say, "How Muslims deal with the political opposition.") The story I want to tell you about has to do with a Jewish woman named Um Kurfa. She was a poet, one hundred and twenty years old, who recited a poem about the Prophet that he took objection to. So he killed her. The one who claimed to come bringing mercy to all people caught her and tied her legs to two different camels. Then he forced the camels to go in opposite directions. This is how she died – torn in two. No one would dare to say anything against him. You are free to consider how disgusting this story is.

There are many, many unanswered questions in the Quran. Space does not permit me to mention more than these few.

I continued to practice all the things my religion required of me, not out of love for God, but in fear of him. God, as described in the Quran, is the greatest, the strongest, the avenger. I used to practice my religion so God wouldn't be angry with me.

More Than A Dream

While studying science at university in Nineveh in northern Iraq, I began to meet people of different religions. Some of them were Christian. One mathematics classmate was very kind and loving. I used to enjoy being with him, except that he was Christian. We Muslims believe Christians are second-class citizens and that we shouldn't be their friends so, despite liking him, I tried to avoid him.

After I graduated from university in 1993, my faith in Islam fell apart. All the time I had spent searching for the God of Islam amounted to nothing. Through my study of the history of Islam, I came to the conclusion that Islam was a religion created by a few leaders who then used force to spread their ideas. People had no real choice: either become Muslim or be killed.

I concluded that there was no God. I no longer believed he existed or that there was anything that is heavenly. I became an atheist, no longer believing in God. Instead, I began to seek pleasure in the world.

Now it is true that I had given up on God, but at the same time I couldn't enjoy life. I felt depressed and lacked inner peace. I was lost, without hope of finding a new life. All of this weighed me down. I developed a bad attitude toward people around me, including my brothers and friends. I became very depressed, so pessimistic that I considered committing suicide.

Such an idea might scare some people, but it wasn't frightening to me. All the people around me thought that if I committed suicide, I'd go to hell. But I would just laugh at them – if I didn't believe in God, why would I believe in hell?

At this time, God prompted some friends and family to convince me to travel outside Iraq. They were hoping that changing location, job and culture might help to change my frame of mind and cause me to stop thinking such dark thoughts.

Actually, I did travel. I went to Jordan, the only place available for Iraqis at that time. I arrived there in July 1999. God's plan was waiting for me there.

Muhammad Al-Hallaj

Finding My Way to God

When I reached Amman, I began looking for a teaching position at a university - any university. Although I had an advanced degree in science, after six months I hadn't found a thing and the money I had brought was running out. So I began looking for any kind of job to cover my expenses. Finally I found a job working for a company.

The owner of the company had a private library full of books that are forbidden in Muslim countries. These books explained how Islam started and where it came from. They taught how Muhammad married the cousin of Waraqa bin Nuwafal, the priest of a church near Mecca at the time. The church had been expelled from the Eastern Orthodox Church for teaching that Christ was not God, only a prophet from God who did many miracles. Muhammad "borrowed" this heresy and many other stories about the Jewish prophets, and they were all included in the material finally collected in the Quran.

The forbidden books also revealed that Islam started as a tolerant religion that respected other religions in Mecca. In the early stages of Islam, Muhammad endorsed freedom and did not force people to believe as he did. But after relocating in Yethrib (renamed Madina Munawara) and gaining political and military power, he refashioned Islam into a dictatorial religion that killed anyone who opposed it.

When I read this uncensored history, the scales fell off my eyes. When I thought back on the years I'd spent searching for God in Islam, I realized that I didn't have peace within Islam because it isn't really a religion from God. This realization gave me hope that God might really exist – but where and how could I find him? That is when I remembered my Christian friend who had studied with me at the university. Back then I had refused to let myself get close to him, but I remembered his kindness and that I had admired the way he lived. I wondered about the Christian Quran (I didn't know at that time that it was called the Holy Bible), which was my friend's holy book.

I started searching for books about Christianity. I read some from the library but found they presented only a negative reading of Jewish and Christian history. These books were not useful to me because I was looking for books about the religion itself, not its history. My goal was to find God. I reasoned that I might find helpful books about the Christian religion in a Christian bookstore.

I located a bookstore, bought a few short books and began reading. There were many concepts I didn't understand, like the "Holy Spirit" and "God is one in three persons". Because I had spent most of my life in a Muslim culture studying Islamic history and the Quran, Christian vocabulary and jargon were completely foreign to me. I asked for help from a co-worker whose name indicated that he was Christian. We met and I asked him many questions. He told me he didn't have answers for me, but maybe I could go to a church and someone there would answer my questions. He encouraged me and finally convinced me to give it a try.

After a number of days I started looking for a church. In the middle of Amman, I found a big church with high spires and a large cross on top of it. I became fearful the moment I stepped inside. I was met by a person wearing a black robe and a black hat. He wore a cross around his neck and had a big beard. When I saw him I thought he must be the Imam of the church. I introduced myself to him saying, "I am Muhammad al-Hallaaj." I told him about my background and that I'd come to the church searching for God. "Can you explain what God means to you? How do you envision God? Is he a great avenger? Or is he kind and merciful?" I asked my questions and waited for him to answer.

I was not expecting the kind of response he gave me! He told me to leave the church and not come back again! Why? What did this answer mean? I was speechless. I left feeling very embarrassed and very angry. Since I had never in my life discussed anything with an Imam, after this Imam's disheartening response, I could not reply.

I went back to my co-worker who had sent me to church and unleashed my fury on him. As I swore at him he just stood there smiling at me to disarm my anger. When I cooled down he explained to me, "This priest was afraid of you because he thought you were working with the secret police. God has a purpose even in this." I asked him, "What do you mean?" He told me, "That kind of church is very traditional. It won't help you to search for God in that kind of place. They are like Islam in that there are many layers of holy people between you and God. They changed the saints who were humble servants of Christ into great men and forgot Christ's teaching that everything we ask, we should ask in Christ's name. Those people put their saints in the place of God."

Then my friend gave me good news: he promised to take me to a church where I would find God. He took me to an evangelical church. April of 2000 was the first time I saw the inside of a church. I listened to the music. There were beautiful hymns and I enjoyed the worship very much. When the pastor started to preach, something amazing happened. Every word he spoke seemed to be intended for me! At least that's how I felt. I wondered deep in my heart how he knew that I was visiting the church for the first time. How did he know that I was searching for God? I thought perhaps my friend had told the pastor about me, but later he assured me that this was not the case. The message that day was God's special Word to me. God spoke to me through that pastor.

At the end of the service I approached the pastor, introduced myself and told him about my background and what I believed. I told him I was searching for God in his religion, Christianity. I was prepared that, when I finished, he also might tell me to leave and never come back. Instead he said, "Welcome! This is God's house. You are welcome any time." He gave me a Bible. In Islam I had been forbidden to read or even touch a Bible. This was the first time I'd ever touched a Bible, and when I did, something strange happened inside me. I felt a tingle in my spine and peace in my soul. And from that time I started to walk in God's way.

Muhammad Al-Hallaaj

Beginning To Walk With Christ

In the first few days after beginning to walk with God, I came up against many difficulties! I began to experience health problems. I almost lost my job and had some economic concerns. Several relationships became unexplainably difficult. At first I thought that God was punishing me for leaving Islam and following Christianity. When I shared my problems with some other believers, they told me I was experiencing opposition from satan, not God. He was determined to keep me from continuing in God's way. They prayed with me and the problems disappeared! My God proved himself to be the most powerful.

Although I worked eleven-hour days, I still went to church every night after work. On Sunday, I went to the worship service, on Monday there was a special service, and on Wednesday and Thursday nights there were Bible studies. On Friday, my day off, I went to one service for African believers and a different meeting in the evening. On Saturday evening I participated in a home Bible study. Every day I could attend a service at a different evangelical church.

From the first day I had a Bible I started reading eagerly at home every night. I would take the Bible to bed and read it under my blanket because I was afraid my housemates, two Muslim men, might see me with it. Though I was physically tired from the long workday, I loved reading the Bible. After studying the Bible for some time, I realized where eighty per cent of Islamic laws come from: they were borrowed from the Bible, especially the Old Testament.

This was my life from April 2000 until November 2001. During that time I still had not accepted that Christ is God, and that He is alive and at work today. Even though I didn't believe, I kept going to church, and I felt peace in my heart for the first time in my life. The people in the church were very kind to me. Most of them didn't know that I was from a Muslim background because I'd asked the pastor not to tell anyone. Because I was born Muslim, I was still considered a Muslim, and I lived in a Muslim country. I had reason to fear Muslims finding out that I attended church every day.

Muhammad Al-Hallaj

Spiritual Transformation

One day in November of 2001 I developed a problem with my health. I had severe pain in the right side of my stomach and my whole body felt tired. I assumed the tiredness was because I worked such long hours and then went to church after work every day – my body should be tired! But this particular evening, when the pastor asked during his message for anyone needing special prayer to come to the front, I was the first person in line. I really needed special prayer for my health. A group of people joined me in the line. I raised my hands and closed my eyes and began talking to God. I felt someone put a hand on my shoulder but the sensation was not the same as when the pastor had prayed for me before. The moment I felt the touch on my shoulder, my stomach pain disappeared. I began to feel a transformation come over my body. It was as if a stone statue was becoming human. All my tiredness and sickness vanished. Something cool was going through my body, yet I was sweating. I felt refreshed. It was a wonderful feeling. Afterward it seemed that I had a new body.

I even felt a change in my thinking – my pessimistic, black thoughts disappeared. I felt like my mind was undergoing an operation to cleanse it of all evil thoughts until I felt spiritually refreshed and had right thoughts inside my mind and soul. For the first time in my life I didn't feel stressed. I had wonderful peace inside me. Suddenly I realized my old, heavy heart had been taken away and replaced with a new one full of peace and love. This was a completely new experience.

The whole process seemed to take about ten minutes. After that, my hands and legs started feeling tired. I couldn't hold my hands high any longer and wanted to put them down. I was uncomfortable about the pastor taking so much time with me while the others were standing there waiting, so I opened my eyes. There was no one near me! The pastor was at the other end of the church. Then I realized that it had been the glorious Lord Jesus Christ who had placed his hand on my shoulder. His touch had healed me and given me a new heart, a new mind and new life.

After that night my life changed completely. I was no longer lost, without purpose or hope. Every morning when I woke up my heart and mind were flooded with joy and peace. Even the people I dealt with every day noticed the significant change that had happened in me. They could sense the powerful peace that was overflowing in my life.

The way I read the Bible started to change too. I used to read it as a story or as history. After that night of transformation, I started reading the Bible with the Holy Spirit's help and understanding it from God's perspective. I marveled at how the things that used to be the hardest to make sense of - such as the Trinity - became simple to me now. I became confident in my faith and began telling people outside the church that I was a believer. I would tell them the story of what had happened to me. At the same time, I was cautious and refrained from sharing my story with some people. You could say my faith was like the faith of a child. I started growing in my faith through continually practicing prayer to God, fellowship with believers, Bible reading and Bible study.

Muhammad Al-Hallaaj

Abu Abdullah and the Voice of God

I used to walk through downtown on my way to work. I would see a homeless man who lived on the sidewalk. I wanted to speak to him but was afraid he might not welcome me. One day as I was going to the bookstore I noticed him sitting on the corner. This time, when I looked at him I heard a voice telling me to go and tell him about God. I wasn't sure it was God's voice I had heard. What would God want with a homeless man? He has mental problems! How would he understand the love and redemption of Christ? I acted like Jonah and ran from my duty, escaping to the other side of the road. Then the voice of God came again and this time more clearly: "Go and tell him, 'Christ loves you!'"

At that point, I had no choice. I went back to him, wondering how I was going to tell this man about the love of Christ. There was a sweets shop on the corner. I went in and bought some sweets. I put them on a plate, walked over and sat next to him on the street. He looked at me strangely. I gave him the sweets and told him, "This is from

Jesus Christ, the son of Mary. He loves you." He took the plate, threw away the spoon, and started eating with his hands. He kept saying, "Yes, and I love him. I love him."

I looked around wondering what more I should say. I couldn't think of anything. I stood up and started to walk away from the man. Suddenly someone near us grabbed my arm. He had been standing near us and overheard me talking to the homeless man. "Are you Christian?" he asked.

I hesitated. Then I responded, "That depends. If you're from the secret police, I'm a Muslim. If you aren't, then I'm a Christian."

He laughed and answered, "Don't be afraid. I don't work for the government. But I have a question for you."

"Ask it," I responded.

He said, "Every day we Muslims abuse you Christians and say your God is just a prophet who comes after our prophet. In many Islamic countries, you don't have rights. And you don't protest. But in many countries, after the cartoon appeared in the newspaper in Europe making fun of our prophet Muhammad, we Muslims demonstrated and burned embassies, and if we had had the chance we would have killed some of you. Why do you Christians take all we do and keep quiet and not fight for your rights?"

Honestly, I liked this question. I answered him from the Bible, "Do not take revenge, my friends, but leave room for God's wrath, for it is written: It is mine to avenge; I will repay, says the Lord."[5] Also, God said, "Love your enemy."

---

[5]Romans 12:19

The man was astonished at my response and asked, "How can you love those who hurt you and insult you and dislike you? That is something strange."

I tried to explain to him that we don't have a choice to love them or not. "Jesus taught us clearly that we must love our enemies and also pray for them. God instructed us and he knows that we cannot do this by ourselves without his help. This is why we need to ask God for help. We need to be made into his image and to live as Jesus did."

I didn't have time to continue the conversation since I needed to return to work. But I sensed he wanted to talk more. I apologized to him and suggested he meet me there again at 8:00 after I had finished work. Later I found him there, waiting for me. Abu Abdullah and I went to my home and talked until 11:00 pm. He liked what I told him and he asked for a copy of the Bible. I offered to pray for him, which he accepted.

As I prayed for him, God gave me a special word to pray for this man.

> *"Lord Jesus, Lord of glory, it is easy for me to behave in front of people, but you are the God who examines our hearts and you know what's inside every human heart. The heart is the wellspring of good or evil and I can't hide anything from you. Help me, God, to change into the image that you portrayed with your life on the earth, a life without sin and full of obedience and love. I know that I can't do this alone. But I ask you, Lord, to help me to walk in the way of love and to invest my life testifying about your love. To you be all the glory forever. Amen."*

When it was time to go, I walked my friend to the door. He was very relaxed. At the door, I automatically I handed him my card. Usually I keep handy a small piece of paper with my name and phone number on it so anyone who might have questions or wants to hear more about Christ can call me. But this time, without thinking, I handed him my business card that had my name "Muhammad Al-Hallaaj" on it. When he read the name he asked, "Who is Muhammad Al-Hallaaj?" I told him it was my name.

He was taken aback and said, "How can you be a Christian and preach about Christ when your name is Muhammad?" Then he stopped and quietly said, "Good night."

A little while after he left, my doorbell rang. When I opened the door it was Abu Abdullah again. Perplexed, he said to me, "If you are a Christian and you talk about Christ, how nice and ordinary this would be. I would have gone home happy. But you are a Muslim. Why do you talk like this? What happened to you? This is the question I would love to know – what happened in your life?"

I welcomed him back into my home and we stayed up talking until 2:30 am. He accepted Jesus as his savior and went home in peace. Ten days later, Abu Abdullah called to say goodbye to me. He was returning to his country. I was surprised and asked him,

"Where's your country?"

He told me that he was from Saudi Arabia and he had come to Jordan because his daughter needed an operation on her heart. The operation had been performed already and was successful. It was time for him to return to his country. I have never heard from Abu Abdullah since then.

Can you perceive the miraculous pathway of God? First he used the sickness of Abu Abdullah's daughter to bring him to Jordan. Then he used a homeless man sleeping on the sidewalk – a man I'd seen daily for five years and had never thought to even come near him! But God used that homeless man so Abu Abdullah would hear the message of God's love. And he used my name "Muhammad" to stir up questions in Abu Abdullah's heart, so much so that he came back to find out what had happened in my life and surrendered his life to Jesus Christ, the God of glory!

I am convinced that God has a special plan to glorify himself uniquely in each person. Do you want to see the God of glory at work in your life? Ask, my dear brother and sister! For the Lord of glory says, "Ask in faith!" Ask the Lord of glory to show you the right path! I am not asking you to change your religion. No, my dear brother and sister, let the Muslim stay a Muslim, and the Christian stay a Christian, and the Sikh a Sikh and the Jew a Jew. Don't concern yourself with changing your religion; instead, seek to grow in your relationship with God.

Sit alone and talk with the Lord as a friend or a father – or whichever of his characteristics means the most to you. Ask him to show you his glory in your life. Believe me, because I am talking about a life I live every day, even every moment. When God's glory appears in your life, you will know the true meaning of peace and love and you will want only to love and love and love. Imagine with me how life will taste when you live in love. I will pray for you now, and you can pray these words with me, and I am certain that God will hear your prayer.

Muhammad Al-Hallaaj

"Thank you, Lord, for loving all sinners of which I am the first. I thank you for being the good shepherd and taking care of us – even the smallest details of our lives matter to you. Help me, Lord, to be free from sin. I believe Jesus died for my sin. Thank you, God, for forgiving my sins through him and saving me from the world's control over my soul. Help me to see your glory and to touch and taste your peace in my life. Now I want to live my life for you and to show your love to those who want to do me harm. I'm confident that you hear me, Lord. I give you all the glory. Amen."

Muhammad Al-Hallaaj

The Trials of My Faith

Through the Lord's grace, I became a reason for rejoicing in heaven as it says in his Word, "There is rejoicing in the presence of the angels of God over one sinner who repents."[6] God is sovereign and knows all that will happen. He used all the time I had spent searching for him in the Quran and Islam to teach me something valuable. After I saw his light and believed, the knowledge I had gained from reading so many books on Islam and Christianity made it easy for me to talk with Muslims. I have been able to lead some lost sheep into Christ's sheep pen using the Quran and books about Christ.

But the fruit of my walk with Jesus upset the devil and he wasn't happy. He tried to use his forces to stop my ministry. One day I sat with a Shiite Muslim, sharing with him the message of love and what my life had been like before I came to know the God of glory. I described how my life was filled with peace and joy and told him the message of salvation. This man was listening to me on the outside, but inside he was furious with me, and plotting against

[6] Luke 15:10

me. After a few days he returned to Iraq and reported our conversation to a group called the "Mahdi Army" or "Jaysh Al-Mahdi", a Shiite extremist group led by Muqtadi Sadr, that follows the teaching of the Sadri party.

The Islamic way of ruling is to pass the leadership on to your son when you die. The former leader, Muqtadi Sadr's father, had been a prominent religious leader, but this son is nothing like his father was. He molded the group of ignorant, impressionable young people in the party into a gang of terrorists who harass, rob and kill people. They have substantial influence in many Middle Eastern countries, including Jordan. After the man I'd been sharing with told them about me, they called me on my mobile phone to threaten me. They told me they knew all about the church I attended and all the people I was meeting with. They told me I had two weeks to return to Islam.

The call didn't really surprise me. I was living and working in a Muslim country among Muslim people, and my name is Muhammad. From the time I became a Christian and started attending church, choosing to live my life as a follower of Jesus, I expected that one day I would face difficulties and hear words I didn't like.

Three weeks later, three men came to my office and asked to speak with me. They introduced themselves as members of the same group that had called me. They told me they were watching every step I took. They knew everywhere I went and everyone I met with. They accused me of continuing to go to church and of telling people about Christ. I tried to defuse their anger toward me for being a backslider from Islam, but to no avail. Then I tried to finish the conversation quickly, but they promised to enforce Sharia law against me if I continued to follow Christ. This warning was even more serious than before because it meant they would kill me. This was no joke! Three really bad men were standing in my office threatening me. To be honest, I was afraid.

I was afraid not just for me but also for my brothers from Muslim backgrounds whom I was accustomed to visiting. I was afraid they and their families would be harmed. I shared with the pastor of my church and some of my friends what had happened. I stopped visiting certain people to protect them from this terrorist group. But I kept going to church because I couldn't stay away from the fellowship of believers very long.

One evening about a month after the visit in my office, I finished work and went home. At about nine o'clock the doorbell rang. I wondered who it might be, since I wasn't expecting anyone and no one had called to say they were coming over. I thought it might be my landlord or one of my neighbors. When I opened the door, a stranger was standing there. He asked, "Are you Mr. Muhammad Al-Hallaaj?" I told him I was and he said, "Can I take two minutes of your time to talk?"

It was difficult for me to say no because he was speaking so kindly. In our Arab culture, we are supposed to receive visitors, so I invited him in. Suddenly four other men, who'd been standing around the corner so that I did not see them at first, burst into my home with the first man. Taken by surprise, I told these four to leave, but the first man told me, "We only want to talk to you."

I had no choice but to let them in, so I asked them to sit down and offered them something to drink, which they refused. The leader of the group told me, "We called you once on your mobile phone and next we sent people to your office." I realized these men were from the Mahdi Army. He continued, "We gave you a chance to repent and return from backsliding, but you didn't listen to us. The Shiite Court held a session at the Shiite Academy in Iraq and decided to execute you in accordance with Sharia law." He took out a document and read the court order to me. It said that if I continued to walk in violation of Islam, I must be killed. It referenced several Quranic verses about slicing the necks of backsliders, a penalty also supported by the hadiths of the prophet Muhammad as well as some Shiite holy men. In the end I was given one choice: declare my repentance, declare the three witnesses of Islam,[7] and pray with them to ask for forgiveness from God. They said it was up to me –these things I must do or I would die.

I said to them, "I don't deny what you said because I know that's the way you think you can please God, but when you came in you said you wanted to talk. So let's talk. Now ask me why I left Islam. Ask me why I chose to follow Christ. What did I find with Christ I didn't find in Islam? Ask me these questions and let's talk about Christ from the Quran you believe in." (From my studies of the Quran,

[7] Sunnis have only two witnesses.

I knew that the greatest person mentioned there is Christ. I wanted to explain to them through the Quran that Christ is the Spirit of God and the Word of God.)

They didn't want to hear what I had to say and were afraid to debate with me. The leader refused to discuss anything. He insisted, "We came to execute the decision and not to debate." I tried to get them to talk, but they had come only to kill me. Finally I got tired of arguing. I realized my only option was to try to run away from the apartment, but this wasn't going to be easy with five killers surrounding me. I tried to run anyway, but they were ready for me. They grabbed me and pinned me to the floor on my back. Two of them stood on my knees, immobilizing my legs. It felt like my knees were going to break under their weight. Two others spread my arms out and stood on them. I couldn't move at all. The leader took out a knife. He placed his foot on my head and forced my face to look toward the Kaaba in Mecca, as is required whenever Muslims slaughter an animal.

As he pushed on my head with his foot, I cried out, "Where are you, Lord?" With my face turned to the side, all I could see was the carpet. Suddenly the surface of the carpet transformed into something like a shining lake and I saw the glory of God, Jesus Christ, walking on the surface of the water. His face was handsome and he had a pleasant smile. The moment I saw his face, I no longer felt any pain and the fear in my chest became a kind of peace I had never experienced in seven years of walking with Jesus. Every moment of that seven years I had been living in grace and peace with him, but seeing him face-to-face in that moment – this peace was ever so much more! It was beyond human expression.

From the moment I had seen Jesus all the pain had disappeared, so I thought they must have slit my throat and I was already with Christ in heaven. Then Jesus said to me, "Don't be afraid. They can't do anything to you." I realized I was still in the world. I called out and asked Jesus to take me with him. I told him I didn't want to stay in this world having tasted the peace that comes in his presence. I pleaded, "Please Lord, take me with you! I don't want to go back to the world."

I was waiting to feel the knife on my neck, but they seemed to be taking so much time! Why didn't they kill me? I opened my eyes and saw that they had stepped back from me. They looked terrified. I wondered what had happened to these men. I was still lying on the floor, unable to speak. Their leader addressed me in a shaky voice, "We'll give you two more weeks. You should leave Jordan." And then they rushed out. What had happened to them? What had they seen that made them abandon their mission and leave me unharmed?

It all seemed like a dream or a vision. I lay on the floor experiencing two overwhelming feelings. First, I was glad to be alive! Second, I was dismayed that the brief face-to-face encounter with Jesus had ended! Soon I felt encouraged enough to get up, ready to accept whatever might happen to me. I could fully appreciate what the Lord had meant when he said, "whoever touches you touches the apple of my eye".[8] Indeed, this was an experiential and miraculous way for God to show how he cares for his children.

[8] Zechariah 2:8

From that night on, the enemy of all that is good, the devil, had a big problem with me. After I had experienced God's amazing ability to take care of me, I stopped being afraid of the world and was filled with great courage to share more with others the message of love and salvation. The devil lost when he used his servants, the Mahdi Army, to try to get me to betray the righteous way. A few weeks later, there would be another round with the enemy and a different army.

Great Joy

Some of you will have heard about how the secret police in developing countries treat people. The trampling of human rights is especially true in the Arab world. There are many known cases of people being taken by the secret police only to "disappear" and never be heard from again.

One morning when I took a taxi to work I spoke to the driver about what God had done in my life and how I had been saved from the clutches of death. I had one copy of the Bible with me and gave it to him as a gift. When we arrived at my office, I gave him my card in case he had any questions. Reading the card he saw my name and asked, "How is that you are a missionary preaching about Christ and your name is Muhammad Al-Hallaaj? How can you do this when you're Muslim?"

I explained to him, "Christ is for everyone and the people who need Christ in their lives the most are Muslims. Christ said, 'It's not healthy people who need a doctor, but the sick.'[9] That's why we need him more than anyone else." It happened that the taxi driver

[9] Mark 2:17

was working with the secret police. The next day the secret police came to my office and arrested me. They put me in a small cell at the jail. The enemy of the good began to invade my mind with images of myself being tortured. He revealed how they would take off my fingernails and burn my back with their cigarette butts, and many other things. In all these images, I saw happening to me the worst things we have heard about how the secret police handle prisoners underground and in secret.

To break the devil's spell over me, I tentatively began singing some hymns. The first song came out weakly with a trembling voice, but after a few words a strange power and great joy came over me. I began to sing louder, to the point that one of the police guards became irritated and shouted at me to keep quiet. But I didn't stop – I kept singing! I didn't know where this joy and peace had come from so suddenly. Usually in this sort of situation people are afraid, but I was not afraid. I found out later that at that same moment many believers were praying for me. The peace and joy I was experiencing was the fruit of their prayers. This is what the Bible tells us, to pray for one another.

I was held in jail for five days. The first day I was interrogated for eight hours. Even though the officer's tone was threateningly vicious, I had no fear at all. The whole thing didn't seem serious to me. At the end of five days, they hadn't been able to accomplish anything with this "crazy man who loved Jesus." They decided to send me back to Iraq. The officer insisted I return overland even though I'd asked to go by plane at my own expense. At that time the highway from the Jordanian border to Baghdad was controlled by Al-Qaeda. He was probably hoping I would be murdered by Al-Qaeda[10] on the way. They put me in an SUV for the nine-hour journey to Baghdad. At the border crossing between Jordan and Iraq the Jordanians fingerprinted me, scanned my eyes and put a red stamp in my passport. Then they pointed me to the east and said, "Go to Iraq. Get away from here."

[10] Al-Qaeda carries the message of death to the world. Their god rejoices when they kill.

Muhammad Al-Hallaj

Angels Drive Hummers

It was dark, but I wasn't sure what time it was. I began walking into Iraq. After about one and a half hours I reached the first Iraqi border checkpoint. They welcomed me but were wondering why I was walking along this dangerous road alone so late at night. There are many scorpions, snakes and hyenas in that area. Honestly, when they told me this, I agreed that it wasn't safe for anyone to walk in this area. But I wasn't surprised that I had had such peace walking this long distance without any problems. I knew God was with me, protecting me, as usual.

My goal was to return to my family. There were two impossible routes. The first was to go through the town of Fallujah, which at that time was an Al-Qaeda stronghold. Obviously, I couldn't use that route. The second way was to go south, but this road went through several areas controlled by the Mahdi Army – the very people who had tried to kill me before.

I lingered at the Iraqi border for two days waiting for God to show me how to return to my family. I prayed constantly, asking the

Lord of glory to show me his will. "Why did you allow me to leave Amman? I'm sure that no one could have taken me from there without your permission. Show me what you want me to do, O Lord!"

After two days at the border, two men approached me and asked if I would like to go with them to Damascus, the capital of Syria. I wondered about this. I had been asking God to show me the way to return to my family. Was it his will that I should go to Syria? I asked them to give me five minutes and went off by myself. I knelt down and prayed, asking God for his guidance. I sensed him answering me, "Yes, go."

At this point we had to deal with the challenge of finding a car to take us from the Iraqi-Jordanian border to the Iraqi-Syrian border. After some time we found a car willing to take us to the Syrian border, but the driver said we must drive 150 km east toward Fallujah and then go 170 km northwest toward the Syrian border. The entire area we would drive through was full of Al-Qaeda militia. It is well known that members of Al-Qaeda are eager to kill anyone who isn't from the Wahabi sect

– this was reason enough for them to kill us. If we were caught, they would chop off our heads. I told the driver not to be afraid, as this was not going to be a problem for us. The driver looked at me and said, "What do you mean it won't be a problem?"

I said to him, "This is God's problem. He's the one who told me go to Syria. My life is in his hands and he will take care of it. This is one of his mercies to us. We need to trust in him and obey." The driver gave me a look like I was crazy, but he started driving us toward the Syrian border.

Imagine, we had just begun driving to Syria and had not even gone one kilometer on the highway when we were surrounded by three Hummers of the type usually used by the American army. They had guns mounted on top and were driving parallel to us at a distance of only about one hundred meters. We saw them all of a sudden, without any warning. Everybody knows that when another car approaches you on the highway, it begins as a small point in the distance and slowly increases in size as it catches up to you. Then you can see the actual size of the car. This is logical. But what happened with these Hummers was not logical – they appeared instantly. We were in a deserted area and none of us had seen them coming. We all wondered where they had come from. Their appearance helped me feel safe from Al-Qaeda, at least for the time being.

The Hummers continued driving toward the east alongside us until we reached the crossing where we needed to turn toward the Syrian border. Miraculously, they turned with us. Just as we reached the Syrian border, they suddenly disappeared. We didn't see any dust or any other trace of them. The person sitting next to me was stunned and cried out, "What happened? Where did these people go? What does this mean?" As for me, I was laughing. I knew that these soldiers weren't human, but were angels sent to protect me, his son. This made me feel very special in God's eyes.

We arrived at the Syrian border. One of the men traveling with me noticed the red stamp the Jordanian secret police had put in my passport. He complained angrily, "You should have told me at the Jordanian border that you have a problem with the Jordanian government." I wondered why he needed to know that. What difference would it make? He answered, "Arab countries have their differences with each other, but when it comes to the secret police they cooperate with each other. If you have a problem with the Jordanian secret police, you'll have problems with other Arab countries and your name will be blacklisted."

Again I explained, "This isn't a problem for me. God will take care of it. When I prayed and asked him, he told me to go. This is why I know God can handle this situation."

The man mocked my faith. Together, we went into the office of the border police. There were four policemen taking passports. We went to the first window. The first of our group presented his passport with fifty US dollars tucked inside. All Iraqis have to pay this amount to gain entry into Syria. He received a visa with permission for a two-week visit. The second person did the same and received a two-week visa. When my turn came, I handed the officer my passport. I had one hundred dollars in my pocket that I was ready to give him if he asked for it. I was expecting him to look at the red stamp and tell me they didn't like troublemakers. At the very least, I thought he would send me to his supervisor for questioning.

What happened next was something I couldn't have imagined! After he took my passport he started talking to the police officer next to him. He opened my passport but didn't look at my picture as is customary at the border. He didn't even look at the expiry date on the passport. He opened to an empty page and put the visa stamp in. It was a one-month visa! I couldn't believe what I saw! The two men who paid money received two-week visas, but I paid nothing and was given one month! How great is our God!

Muhammad Al-Hallaaj

I crossed over into Syria where I was to live for one and a half wonderful years. It was there that God fulfilled a promise he had given me. But what was God's word to me? What was the promise he fulfilled to me in Syria?

Muhammad Al-Hallaaj

God's Promise Fulfilled

I had been living in Jordan for eight years. During that time I couldn't visit my family in Iraq and they couldn't visit me in Jordan. The Jordanian government had placed severe restrictions on Iraqis wanting to come into the country. Only Iraqis belonging to the previous Baath government or who had become millionaires by robbing banks when the American forces entered Iraq were permitted to enter. My family, not belonging to either of these groups, could not come to visit.

Life had been difficult for me in Jordan. I couldn't marry a Christian believer because my official documents said I was from a Muslim background. If I married, under the law my children would be considered Muslims. It would be impossible to find any Christian who would allow his grandchildren to be considered Muslims. Even if I found a Muslim girl who understood my situation and was sympathetic, her family would refuse me because I was a backslidden Muslim. There was no way to solve this problem. I abandoned any plan to get married and raise a family. I had to stop focusing on earthly matters while in Jordan.

There was always a special meeting on New Year's Eve at the evangelical church I attended in Amman. We would pray for God's blessing in the coming year and to win new souls to Jesus Christ. At our celebration of the New Year of 2007, in the midst of all my difficulties, God spoke to me and promised me that I would enjoy many blessings in my life in 2007.

So what happened that year and how had I experienced God's blessings? Terrorists from the Mahdi Army had tried to kill me, I was arrested and spent time in jail and I had to flee to Syria with a few clothes and little else! Sometimes I was confused by my situation and wondered, "What is going on? Where is the blessing God promised me for 2007?"

Indeed, God poured out his blessing after I entered Syria! While my family had been restricted from entering Jordan, it was easy for them to come to Syria. We were reunited after eight years of not seeing each other. When my siblings returned to Iraq, my mother stayed and lovingly cared for me for a year and a half. And after I had accepted I would have to live as a bachelor for the glory of Christ, God gave me a wife! I could never have dreamed or imagined a better or more beautiful or more amazing wife. She is the one whom Solomon said is "worth more than pearls".

In Jordan I had been too busy with other things to be involved in full-time ministry, but God opened the doors wide for effective ministry in Syria. Syrians understand religion. Because the country has had a long history with Christianity, Syrians are more open-minded than any other people in the Middle East, and they are more receptive to his blessings. God has used the turmoil in Iraq to bring many Iraqis to Syria for a plentiful harvest among them. God gave me favor in the eyes of many of these people. We visited some who were far from the Lord and brought them into his kingdom. They have become followers of Christ and serve him even now in Syria.

My life truly reflects the verse that says, "No eye has seen, no ear has heard, no mind has conceived what God has prepared for those who love him".[11] My life has truly become more than a dream! I live with God every day. When I look back and think about my life before I knew Christ, I wonder how I stayed alive all those years. But, unknown to me at the time, he had been preserving my life for his good purposes. With him, my life has been transformed into what can only be described as **more than a dream**!

[11] 1 Corinthians 2:9

THE STORY OF ODAI MUHAMMAD

Now that I've told you the story of God's work in my life, I want to tell you about Odai Muhammad, a friend of mine, who is another picture of God's power. Who is this person?

Muhammad Al-Hallaaj

Odai's Tragedy

I met Odai in Syria. He was a believer in Christ. He had been blind, but God looked after him in his situation and gave him back his sight. How did this happen? Let me briefly tell you his story in his own words. Because he is still serving the Lord Jesus in the Middle East even as I write, his name has been changed and some details left out.

Odai was born a Sunni Muslim in Basra in southern Iraq. He was born into a large family and raised according to the Muslim way. He was unable to finish his studies because of the disruption caused by war in that region; but from the time he was young, he worked to support himself and his family. When his military service was over he began his own business and married his neighbor's daughter. She was from a Shiite background. God blessed them with children. Up to that point, life looked normal for Odai. He had his own business, home and family. Everything was going well.

But in 2002 Odai was afflicted with an illness in his head. At that time proper medical care for his condition was not available in Iraq because of the economic embargo and war. As a result, Odai lost the grace of sight. He changed from being a successful businessman with a family and a stable life to existing as a blind man. His wife ceaselessly looked for help for him in any place she could. They went to many doctors in many different places and each one operated on him. But after undergoing four operations in less than a year, he was left completely blind. He had sold all he owned to finance the operations and treatments and had moved with his family into his parents' home. They gave him one room to live in with his pregnant wife and four children.

Life became very difficult for Odai, especially with all the responsibilities that a growing family entails. After all that had happened to him, he started thinking about relieving his wife and children from their troubles by committing suicide.

The Healing Touch of Christ

At that very difficult time Odai needed some hope. Someone mentioned to him a good surgeon in Baghdad who could help him. Odai and his wife immediately traveled to Baghdad. They met with the surgeon, who was Director of a very busy and well-known hospital. He gave Odai an appointment for an operation on his eyes in two months; but Odai, his wife by his side in tears, begged him for an earlier date. The surgeon relented and gave him a new appointment in just three days' time. The operation had only a forty per cent chance of success, but Odai had nothing to lose. The risk was worth it.

Three days was not enough time for them to go home and return to Baghdad in time for the surgery. They decided to take a room in the hotel closest to the hospital. The first night, Odai asked his wife to pray and to beg all the prophets she knew from the Quran to help with this operation so that it would be the last one he would need. His wife prayed and asked God to help Odai for the sake of all the prophets. Odai was listening and praying in his heart also. When she reached the prophet Jesus, the son of Mary, and prayed in his name, Odai fell into a deep sleep. The last thing he heard was "the name of Jesus the Messiah, the son of Mary." At three o'clock in the morning, his wife went to sleep as well.

Odai was lying on his back in the bed. Suddenly the wall in front of him split in two and a bright light filled the hotel room. He could see the shadow of a man gesturing to him, but he couldn't see his face because the light coming from him was so brilliant. Odai began to scream in fear. The man comforted him, "Don't be afraid. I've come to save you and heal you."

Odai screamed again, "Who are you?"

The man answered, "I've come to save you and heal you." He approached Odai's bed, took Odai in his arms and held him. Immediately Odai felt an incredible peace that he hadn't felt for a long time. Odai wished this man would hold him forever. Then the man put Odai's head onto his pillow, touched his thumb to Odai's eyes and left.

Odai shouted, "Don't leave me! Please don't leave me!"

At this, his wife woke up and assumed Odai was having a nightmare because of his mental anguish. She tried to console him, telling him that this operation would be successful and his sight would be restored. At that very moment Odai was overjoyed to discover that he could already see! He announced to his wife, "I don't need this surgery! I can see!"

At first she thought he had lost his mind along with his sight! To prove he wasn't making it all up, he began to tell her the color of the curtains and the carpet and the sheets. His wife fainted, collapsing on the floor from the shock. When she came to, he told her about the vision he had seen. Then she recalled that as she awoke to his screaming she had seen a light going into the wall – but she thought she had been dreaming because she had awoken so suddenly.

The next day, Odai and his wife returned to Basra. Their family received them joyfully and praised the brilliant surgeon who had healed Odai so quickly. They assumed that he had already had the operation. He explained to them what had happened, about how someone had visited him and touched his eyes and healed him. He said, "This man is truly my savior and healer but I don't even know who he is."

The Path Leading to Life is Difficult and Narrow

After Odai told his family about his vision and how the man had touched his eyes and healed him, his family rejoiced. They said it was the prophet Muhammad who healed him (because they are Sunni Muslims), but his wife's family (who are Shiite) said it must have been Imam Ali. Everybody praised God according to his own beliefs. They accepted what happened to Odai as a miracle.

But Odai didn't trust either of these men they were praising. Even though he had spent his life trying to please them, neither one had ever contributed to his life, especially during his sickness. Neither of these dead people had done anything to help him before God. Odai said, "The man who healed me told me he came to heal and save me. Who could this savior be? Who is this healer?" When he persisted in saying these things, both families became angry with him and began to give him a hard time. As word of it spread, even some extremist Islamic groups like Al-Qaeda[12] and others funded by Iran began to put pressure on him.

[12] Al-Qaeda became more active in Iraq after Saddam Hussein was removed from power by the American army.

All this created a lot of stress for Odai. But he couldn't forget about the person who had given him back his life. He wanted to thank him, but wondered whom to thank. His head was swimming to the point that he almost wished he hadn't been healed! One night when he was sitting in his room, he called out to the unknown healer and pleaded with him, "Please come again. Who are you?"

A few days later, as Odai was walking down the street, he met a friend from a Christian background who congratulated Odai on his healing. "Congratulations!" he said. "I heard that Muhammad healed you."

But Odai answered, "Muhammad wasn't the one who healed me." The Christian friend was startled to hear him say this because everyone was frightened of the Islamic militant groups. By denying that Muhammad had healed him, Odai was endangering himself.

The Christian friend asked, "Who do you think healed you?"

Odai answered, "I don't know, but he said to me that he would save me and heal me. Who is this savior and healer?"

The man said to him, "Go to the church and ask them for a Bible. Read the Gospel and you will find out who this savior is."

Odai rejected his suggestion, saying, "I am Muslim! I can't touch the Bible! It's forbidden!"

At that, they parted and Odai went on his way. That evening, he sat and pondered what the Christian had said. Three days later, earnestly wanting to know who had given his life back to him, he went to the church in the middle of the city. He spoke to a woman who worked there and asked her for a Bible. Fearful, she hesitated. In those days, the Muslim majority in Iraq was persecuting Christians, who numbered only about one hundred thousand. But, God stepped in to accomplish his plan for Odai. It so happened that this woman had heard the story of Odai's healing, so she agreed to give him a Bible. Rather than handing it to him directly, she placed it on the ground and told him that he should take the book after she left. This way, she would not be in danger if he were caught with a Bible.

She went inside, and Odai picked up the book and went home. He sat down with his wife to read the Gospel of Luke. That very night, Odai discovered who had healed and saved him. When he realized who it was, he became so excited that he took hold of the Bible and started jumping up and down.

He called his mother and brothers and sisters to share his joy with them. They found him holding the Bible, raising it high and shouting, "Jesus, Jesus, Jesus! He is the one who healed me!" Their reaction both surprised and disappointed him. Instead of sharing his happiness, they started to beat him and accuse him of abandoning Islam. They tried to kill him, and then threw him and his family into the street. Odai and his family fled far from Basra to a place near the Iraq-Kuwait border. It was an area that was prohibited for groups like the Mahdi Army and the other militant groups who wanted to kill him. He and his family survived by eating food they had scavenged from the trash. In the midst of these adversities, when his wife was six months pregnant, she lost their baby.

Once when Odai was bringing food to his children he was seized by militant Muslims who took him to a remote place with the intention of executing him. They tied his hands behind him and put a loaded gun to his head. The sheikh who was leading the group scoffed, "A bullet costs $1.50 US. This is an expensive price to pay to kill an apostate like Odai! He isn't worth it!" He ordered the militiaman, "Drill a hole in his head instead. It's free!"

Someone brought a drill and plugged it in. For a moment Odai could feel the air from the drill blowing against his face. In a flash he saw the same vision he had seen when Christ touched his eyes and healed him. Instantly the power failed and the drill stopped working! One of the men tried to restart the generator but it was out of fuel. They sent someone to get fuel.

At that moment, a senior Shiite Imam came in and wanted to know what was going on with Odai. They told him what had happened. He reasoned with them "Why do you want to kill him? Write to his family and ask for a big ransom for him. Then you can set him free and try to catch him again. His family will have to pay even more money to save him next time. This way you can get all the money you need."

The group went to Odai's family and demanded a ransom for his life. One of his brothers told the messenger, "Kill him! We don't want him! He has brought shame on our family."

While they were talking, one of Odai's friends overheard their conversation. He spoke quickly: "I will pay $400 if you let him go."

The friend paid $400 and Odai was released. He warned Odai, "They're going to try to catch you again. In the end, they will kill you. You have to get out of Iraq." The man worked to help Odai get a passport.

Odai and his family were able to escape to Syria where they have lived until now. God has used him to help many people in Syria. His life parallels the lives of those who belonged to the first church, and is a model of faith and sacrifice for us today.

We pray for God to use us to spread his kingdom. Amen.

Now to him who is able to do immeasurably more
than all we ask or imagine,

according to his power that is at work within us,
to him be glory in the church

and in Christ Jesus throughout all generations,
for ever and ever!

Amen.

Ephesians 3:20-21 (NIV)

Endnote

If the reader wishes to verify claims I have made about the Quran, Sharia law, Um Kurfa, Muqtadi Sadr and the Mahdi Army, Al-Qaeda or facts about Sunni and Shia Islam, you can research them for yourself, and you will find that what I have said about them is true.

Those who have questions or would like to learn more about Jesus and ... please email the writer at

muhammadalhallaaj@gmail.com

ولي خراف أخر ليست من هذه الحظيرة ينبغي ان آتي بتلك ايضا فتسمع صوتي وتكون رعية واحدة وراع واحد.

يو16:10

محمد الحلاّج

أروع من حلم

الحياة مع الله

تقديم

أن تعبر خلال لحظة واحدة بعد سنوات طويلة من البحث، أن تتغير حياتك كلها بلمسة واحدة، أن تنتقل من الموت إلى الحياة من حياة مليئة بالألم والضياع والحيرة والأسئلة التي بدون أجوبة، من حياة بلا هدف خالية من سلام أو أي طعم له، من حياة ممنوع فيها أن تستخدم عقلك، وتستمر بالبحث رغم ذلك عن الراحة النفسية والسلام النفسي، تبحث في داخل الكتب فلا تجد ما تنشد إليه تبحث داخل جدران المعابد فلا تجد سوى الدماء والروحانيات المزيفة، بعدها تفكر أن تنهي حياتك الخالية من كل شيء لكن أين ستذهب بعد ذلك؟ ايضاً لا تعرف... فما هو الحل؟

إحتاج محمد لسنوات طويلة حتى يعرف الحق، والحق هو الذي حرره، كيف تغيرت حياته بصورة كبيرة إلى حياة مليئة بالحب والفرح والسلام في لحظة واحدة وبلمسة واحدة؟ هذه هي خطّة الله له ولا أحد يستطيع ان يصل لله المحب إلاّ من خلال هذا الطريق.معا سنعرف أيضا صورة أخرى لقدرة الله و كيف لمس

ان محبه الله غير محدودة.. و هو منذ البدء يسعى لضم اولاده الذين خدعهم ابليس، الى خاصته.و يسعي ابليس جاهدا لعرقله هذا السعي بتبديل الحقائق الإلهية باخرى ليحيد بالانسان عن طريق الله بارادته العنيده..يقول الكتاب المقدس في ما مضى كلم الله اباءنا بواسطه الانبياء مرات كثيره و بطرق متنوعه، اما في هذه الايام الاخيره فقد كلمنا في ابنه.

لم يكن أي من محمد أو عدي يعرف السيد المسيح .. و لكن محبه الفادي تدخلت لتشفي وتخلص وتعلن الفداء .لكن يبقى السؤال المطروح هو كيف ألتقي بالرب الإله؟ ونجد الإجابة في وعد السيد " ان تطلبوني من كل قلوبكم تجدوني

اخي و اختي... هل تلبي النداء لك لتنال الخلاص؟؟. تعال إلى مصدر الحب الحقيقي. الحب الذي ظهرَ على الصليب وقدمه يسوع المسيح لأجلك. فقد نزل من السماء وجاء إلى الأرض لكي يحررنا ويروي قلوبنا من فيض حبه الغير مشروط.

الخلفية

إسمي محمد الحلاج ولدت في الشرق الأوسط وفي مدينة بغداد عاصمة العراق من عائلة إسلامية تدين بالمذهب الشيعي[1].

وحين كان عمري تسع سنين إنتقلت عائلتي إلى مدينة "الحلة" وهي مركز محافظة بابل وتبعد حوالي تسعين كيلو مترا جنوب بغداد وتتسم هذه المدينة بأغلبية شيعية حيث كان لي الكثير من الأصدقاء والجيران وجلّهم من الشيعة، لذا نشأتُ وترعرعت على أفكار المذهب الشيعي والذي كنت أؤمن أنه الطريق الوحيد إلى الجنة، حيث كنت أطبق كافة الأمور التي أراها هي الصحيحة،

[1] ومن المعروف أن الإسلام يتكون على العموم من فريقين هما : السنة والشيعة . الفريق الأول "السنة" وهم على أربعة مذاهب رئيسية وهي:" المالكية والحنفية والشافعية والحنبلية"، وهم يطبقون الشريعة التي إستلموها من رجال أخذت المذاهب أسمائها منهم ويحفظونها بدون اي تطوير أو تغيير. والفريق الآخر "الشيعة" وهم يتبعون دائما الإمام، وهو رجل الدين المتفق علية من قبل الجامعة العلمية الشيعية ويتبعونة ويطبقون كل شيء يقوله لذلك تجد أن التشريع في المذهب الشيعي يختلف بإختلاف الإمام الذي يتبعونه.

فأصلي ثلاث مرات يوميا[2]، وايضا صيام شهر رمضان وزيارة الأماكن المقدسة عند الشيعه، وهي قبرالإمام علي في مدينة النجف وهو ابن عم النبي محمد وزوج إبنته فاطمة في نفس الوقت، وهو رجل مقدس عند الشيعة ويعتبرونه هو الباب الذي يدخلون منه الى الجنة وايضا قبري ولديه الإمام الحسين والامام العباس في مدينة كربلاء وعدة قبور أخرى لبعض الأئمة في بغداد ومدينة سامراء ايضا وكلها تعتبر أماكن مقدسة عند الشيعة، وكنت اقوم بزيارات دورية إلى هذه الأماكن

ظنّا مني أنهم يشفعون لي يوم القيامة ويغفرون كل ذنوبي، فإذا رضيَ عنّي هؤلاء الأشخاص يصبح لزاما على الله أن يدخلني الجنة، وهناك أستمتع بكل أنواع الطعام والشراب وأيضا إثنان وسبعون حورية ، وحور عين وولدان مخلدون ...

كنت أؤمن أن الشيعة وحدهم هم الذين سيرثون السماء حين كانت تغذى عقولنا بكل الأفكار التي تؤكد ذلك، كنا نؤمن أن

[2] الأسلام فيه خمسة أوقات للصلاة الفجر والظهر والعصر والمغرب والعشاء لكن الشيعة يدمجون صلاة الظهر مع العصر في وقت واحد وصلاة المغرب مع العشاء في وقت واحد لذا تصبح ثلاث أوقات للصلاة عند الشيعة.

السماء وفيها هناك الله جالس على العرش في يوم القيامة يسألون الشخص هل أنت شيعي: إذا قال نعم يذهب إلى جهة اليمين وهي الجهة التي تؤدي إلى الجنة وأما المذاهب والديانات الأخرى فيذهبون إلى جهة اليسار وهي الجهة الملعونة والتي تؤدي إلى الجحيم ومن ذلك كنّا نعلم أن جهة اليمين مباركة وجهة اليسار ملعونة حيث كان محرما أن نستخدم اليد اليسرى اثناء تناول الطعام لأنها غير مباركة، كان واجبا أن نطلق اللحية دون حلاقة، فالشخص الذي يحلق لحيته لا ينظر الله إلى وجهه يوم القيامة فكنا نترك اللحى رغم حرارة الجو والتي تصل في الصيف ما يفوق الخمسين درجة مئوية وكنا نتندر على بعض الشباب الذي لم ينبت الله لهم لحى ، بكون الله غاضب منهم؟.

كنّا ندرس في المسجد أن السنّة هم" ذيل" أو ذَنب؟ وكنّا نؤمن بذلك، كما كانوا يعلموننا أن المسيحيين لديهم ثلاثة آلهة ،فهم يعبدون إبن الله فالله ليس لوحده فهو لديه زوجة إسمها مريم ولديهم إبن إسمه عيسى وهو الذي يعبده المسيحيين وكان نبيا يهوديا. وحسب ما كتب في القرآن، قد رفعه الله إلى السماء لأنه كان بدون خطيئة وقد حاول اليهود أن يقتلوه فوضع الله

شكل المسيح على شخص آخر فأخذه اليهود وصلبوه ظنّاً منهم أنّه المسيح أمّا المسيح الحقيقي فقد رفعه الله الى السماء .

أمّا اليهود فقد كان مجرد ذكرهم يجب أن يسبقة كلمة أعوذ بالله فقد كنّا نؤمن أن المسيحيين واليهود هم وقود جهنم وقد مسخ الله قوم منهم على شكل حيوانات منها الخنازير لذلك كان الخنزير محرما أكله في الإسلام حسب هذا الإعتقاد، واليهود هم من أكثر الناس عداوة لنا وقتلهم واجب وغير محرّم حيث أنه في يوم ما سيأتي في المستقبل، وكل المسلمين يعدون له، سيشنون حربا على اليهود ويقتلونهم كلهم وتصبح كل الأرض مسلمة؟؟ ولم أعرف حينها لما يجب أن أكره كل العالم لكني كان يجب أن أفعل فهذا هو الدين الذي اعرفه!!.

كانت هناك الكثير من الأشياء التي كنت لا أفهمها في ديانتنا ولكني يجب أن أؤمن بها مثل الزواج المؤقت والذي يسمى عند الشيعة (زواج المتعة) ، وهو زواج شفهي يتم بين الرجل والمرأة فقط بدون اي شهود أو أي إثبات قانوني ويمكن أن يستمر هذا الزواج لمدة ساعة أو ساعتين أو ليلة واحدة أو أي مدة يختارها

الشخصين حيث كان الشيوخ يتزوجون من اي فتاة تعجبهم عن طريق هذا الزواج، لكن في نفس الوقت كانوا يغضبون ويحرّمون على بناتهم أن يتزوجن " متعة" !! فهو حلال لهم وحرام على غيرهم. لكن كون الإمام أو الشيخ هو برتبة الله عند الشيعة فقد كان من المستحيل أن نقول له لماذا؟ فهذا السؤال قد يأخذك إلى الجحيم مباشرة.

بشكل عام لم أكن من الأشخاص الذين يسألون كثيرا في ذلك العمر فقد كنت مثال المسلم الجيد المطيع حيث كنت في أعين الجميع ملتزم ، فهم يرون كل ما اقوم به يكون حسب الشريعة ولكنهم لم يروا ما بداخلي من عدم إقتناع لكل ما اقوم به، لكن هذه هي الطريقة الوحيدة التي اعرفها والتي توصلني إلى الله ومن ثم إلى الجنة حيث المتع التي لا تعد ولا تحصى والمعدّة لنا هناك، حيث عانينا في العراق ولفترات طويلة من الحرمان وعدم توفر الطعام نتيجة الحروب الكثيرة التي كان يخوضها العراق مع دول جارة كأيران والكويت ، وما يتبع ذلك من مشاكل إقتصادية وأيضا بسبب كبر عائلتنا حيث كانت عائلتي تتكون من أحد عشر شخصا حيث كنا نعاني كعائلة أو حتى كشعب من الفاقة وعدم

توفر النقود لشراء الطعام، ولكن في كل هذا كان هناك تعزية لنا ، إذ سنجد في الجنة كل شيء مجاني وكل ما ترغب به نفوسنا مما لذّ وطاب وأيضا الإثنتان وسبعون زوجة العذراء فقد كنا نتصبر على ذلك العيش بالتمني.

لكن السؤال الذي بدأ يقفز في مخيلتي هل فعلا أنا ذاهب إلى الجنة؟؟ بدأ هذا السؤال وعدّة اسئلة أخرى تخطر في مخيلتي الغضة حينما بلغت السابعة عشر أي قبل دخولي الجامعة بسنة واحدة ومن هنا بدأت رحلة البحث عن الحقيقة .

البدايات

كانت بداية البحث عن الحقيقة عندما كنت في مرحلة الدراسة الاعدادية " التوجيهي " حيث كنّا ندرس الدين الإسلامي بالإضافة الى الدروس التي كنت أحضرها في الجامع، ولكن برغم كل ذلك وبرغم إلتزامي بكل ما يوصيني به ديني لم أكن اشعر أنّه يوجد بيني وبين الله علاقة خاصة كنت اشعر أن الله بعيد جدا عني، هو في السماء السابعة، ولم اكن أتصور أنه ممكن ان يهتم بشؤون شخص صغير مثلي، فلم يكن عندي سلام داخلي ولم أعثر على يقين أنّني ذاهب إلى الجنة فقد كنت في خوف مستمر وكنّا دائما ننظر للإمام علي بن ابي طالب ، وهو ابن عم النبي محمد وزوج ابنته على أنه خليفة الله ويجب أن نرضيه، وبعد الإمام علي يوجد سلسلة من الرجال وتبدأ بولدي الامام علي الحسن والحسين وتنتهي بالمهدي المنتظر أو صاحب الزمان ، كما يسميه الشيعة ، وكل هؤلاء كانوا بيني وبين الله وكنّا دائما نعطي المجد لهؤلاء الرجال فلم يكن هناك مجال لوجود الله في حياتي أو قلبي وبعد فترة طويلة من البحث والذي دائما كان يسبب لي المشاكل

مع رجال الدين، لم أستطع أن أجد الله في المذهب الشيعي فكنت أعتقد في النهاية ان السبب هو المذهب الذي تعتنقه عائلتي المذهب الذي تربيت عليه وهو المذهب الشيعي ، لذا غيّرت مذهبي وأعتنقت المذهب السني.

خلق ذلك التغيير لي مشاكل كثيرة كانت أكبرها مع عائلتي وخصوصا والدتي فقد كنت في نظرها كافرا بأعتناقي المذهب السنّي وطردوني من البيت وذهبت لأعيش مع بعض الأقارب وخلال هذه الفترة كنت أعكف على تطبيق التعاليم الجديدة حيث الصلاة خمس مرات في اليوم وليس ثلاثة وكنت أدرس القرآن في الجامع كل يوم بعد صلاة العشاء وإستمر الحال معي نحو سنتين حيث وجدت أنّه لا يوجد إختلاف كبير بين هذه المذاهب فلا يوجد مجال الى الله أيضا والتعظيم يكون لأشخاص ايضا ومثلما الشيعة يعظمون الإمام علي فالسنّة يعظمون عمر بن الخطاب وهكذا.

خلال هذه الفترة كنت أواضب على قراءة الكتب الإسلامية وكنت استقي المعلومات برحلة البحث عن الله ولكن كان هناك إختلاف في المعلومات ، مما أثار الكثير من الأسئلة في داخلي

ولم أجد اي شخص لديه أي جواب على هذه الأسئلة فبمجرد طرح السؤال تتعرض إلى هجوم ويتهمونك بتبني أفكار هدّامة صهيونية ويهودية وكافرة وفي ذلك العمر كنت أخاف حيث كانت من كبرى المشاكل التي يمكن أن أتعرض لها هو أن يغضب مني الإمام لذا كنت آثر السكوت وأبين لهم أني إقتنعت بجوابهم، لكن لغاية الآن لا توجد لدى شيوخ الإسلام اي أجوبة على تلك الأسئلة، وسوف أسرد بعض هذه الأسئلة هنا عسى ولعل أحد الأخوة المسلمين والذين نحبهم بصدق أن يقرأ هذه الأسئلة ويتفكر فعلا بها ويرى هل الإسلام هو الحل فعلا كما يعتقدون؟..

- لنبدأ من كتاب المسلمين المقدس وهو القرآن حيث الفكرة العامة لدى معظم المسلمين هو وجود قرآن واحد لكن الحقيقة هو أنه لغاية الخليفة الإسلامي الثالث "عثمان بن عفان" كان يوجد هناك ما لا يقل عن ثلاثين نسخة من القرآن ويوجد بين هذه النسخ إختلاف لأن كل نسخة كانت عبارة عما جمعه ذلك الشخص الذي يحتفظ بهذه النسخة أمّا كيف ولماذا اصبحت نسخة واحدة، فلكم الحادثة التي كانت السبب .بعدما وصل الجيش الإسلامي إلى أذربيجان كان مع الجنود المسلمين هناك

نسخ مختلفة من القرآن وأحتجت كل مجموعة بما لديها من نسخة وأدعت صحتها مما أثار الخلاف بين الجنود وأدّى إلى لإقتتال بينهم فخاف القائد من الفتنه وكان اسمه حذيفة بن اليمان فذهب هذا القائد إلى خليفة المسلمين آنذاك عثمان بن عفان وشرح له ما حصل فطلب عثمان من الناس أن يجمعوا ما عندهم من نسخ القرآن، وكانت الكتابة في ذلك الوقت على جلود لحيوانات أو على بعض أنواع أوراق الشجر وأيضا كان بعض الناس يحفظون في أذهانهم بعض الآيات ولا يخفى عن الأحبة المسلمين ما كان من خلاف بين الخليفة عثمان بن عفان والعائلات الأخرى بعدما قرب عائلتة وسلمهم الحكم على المسلمين في جميع المدن لتي دخلوها لذلك رفض عبد الله بن مسعود وهو أفضل شخص حسب كتب السيرة في حفظ القرآن أن يسلم نسخته للخليفة وايضا رفض الخليفة نسخة الإمام علي بن أبي طالب لما بين الأمويين والعلويين من خلاف[3] وجمع عثمان بن عفان ما وافق علية صحبة أنه صحيح ورتبوه ترتيب عشوائي وقسموه إلى أقسام

[3] ولهذا السبب يدعي الشيعة لغاية الآن ان لديهم نسخة مصحف خاصّة بهم يسمى مصحف فاطمة

سموها سور[4] وأطلقوا على هذه السور تسميات مختلفة وأطلق على هذه النسخة مصحف عثمان لذى فأن جميع نسخ القرآن الموجودة الآن هي مصحف عثمان ويمكن للأحبة المسلمين أن يفتحوا أول صفحة من القرآن وسيجدوا هذه العبارة "هذا المصحف عن سيدنا عثمان بن عفّان وبرواية حفص" وهي تعني أن هذا المصحف هو برواية شخص اسمه حفص وقد وافق عثمان عليه وطبعه وجعله كتاب رسمي للإسلام؟؟؟" وهنا نسأل عن هذه العبارة والتي كثيرا منهم لم يفكروا ماذا تعني، إذا هذا الكتاب الذي يؤمنون به هو ليس بالضرورة كلام الله فنحن نجد أن بعض الأشعار قبل الإسلام كان فيها الكثير مما يوجد في القرآن ويمكن للأحبة ان يبحثوا عن شعر الكاهن سطيح أو الكاهنة الزبراء وشعر لويس شيخو وغيرهم ممن كتب قبل الإسلام وتعتبر أشعارهم الآن ممنوعة في الدول الإسلامية فلماذا إذاً هو مقدس وكان هذا السؤال الذي حين سألته قامت ثورة في وجهي لم تهدأ إلاّ بهروبي بسرعة من الجامع.

[4] كلمة سورة ليست عربية بل اعجمية سريانية

- سؤال آخر أيضا كان يحيرني حول القرآن والشريعة في الإسلام، فالقرآن يحتوي على ستة آلاف آية ما يتضمن منها تشريعات أو أحكام شرعية في العبادات والمعاملات لا يصل إلى سبعمائة آية منها حوالي مائتي آية فقط هي التي تقرر أحكاما للأحوال الشخصية والمواريث أو للتعامل المدني أي أن الآيات التي تعد تشريعا هي مجرد جزء واحد من ثلاثين جزءاً من آيات القرآن أي (200\6000) وبعض هذه الآيات منسوخة ولا يُعمل بها، أي أن الأحكام السارية أقل من واحد إلى ثلاثين وعلى وجه الدقة هناك ثمانون آية فقط اي (80\6000) أي بنسبة (75:1) ونرى هنا ضعف القرآن في التشريع. السؤال الذي يطرح هنا من اين جاء شيوخ الإسلام بالتشريع وكيف كانوا يحكمون ومن اين كانت كل هذه التشريعات؟

- يدعي المسلمين أن دينهم دين رحمة وأن نبي الإسلام جاء بالرحمة لكنّي لمّا كنت أبحث عن الله في كتب التاريخ الإسلامي كنت أصعق لبعض القصص المرعبة لا اريد ان اسرد جميع أو بعض هذه القصص لكن أكتفي بواحدة هنا وهي تشرح ماذا يحصل للشخص الذي يعارض رئيس الدولة في الإسلام أي

بصيغة المصطلحات الحديثة بماذا أو كيف يعالج الإسلام المعارضة السياسية له؟ القصة التي اريد ان أذكرها هنا هي عن أمرأة يهودية إسمها أم قرفة وكان عمرها مائة وعشرين سنة وكانت شاعرة قالت شعر عن النبي سبب له الكآبة وأزعجه لذا قام بقتلها ،أمّا كيف قتلها النبي الذي يدّعي أنّه جاء بدين رحمة حيث قبض عليها وربط رجليها كل رجل بجمل وساق الجملين بأتجاهين مختلفين وقسمها إلى نصفين لتكون عبرة للجميع، ولك أن تشعر بما تشاء من الأشمئزاز حول ذلك.

ويوجد الكثير الكثير من الأسئلة بدون أجوبة ليس في هذا الكتيب مجالا لطرحها

بعد هذه الفترة والتي كنت أطبق فيها ما يمليه عليّ ديني ليس حبّا في الله لكن خوفاً منه، فالله حسب ما هو موصوف في القرآن هو الجبّار والمنتقم والقهّار لذا كانت علاقتي مع الله علاقة خوف فكنت أطبق ديني حتى أبتعد عن غضب الله منّي ولكن بعد دخولي الجامعة وكنت قد درست العلوم في شمال العراق في مدينة نينوى إلتقيت باناس مختلفين عني منهم الايزيديين والمسيحيين وكان هناك طالب مسيحي يدرس معي في قسم

لرياضيات ، كان هذا الشاب لطيف جداّ وودود وكنت أحب ان
نكون اصدقاء لولا أنّه مسيحي، ففي الإسلام نؤمن أن المسيحيين
أصحاب ذمّة وليسوا أهلا ليكونوا أصدقاءً لنا ! لذا حاولت الإبتعاد
عنه بقدر المستطاع وتحاشي اللقاء به .

بعد تخرجي من الجامعة سنة 1993 أصبحت علاقتي
مع الإسلام سيئة فكل البحث الذي كنت ابحثه عن الله، إله السلام
لم يوصلني إلى شيء ومن خلال دراستي لتاريخ نشأة الإسلام
وصلت لنتيجة مفادها أن الإسلام هو دين وضعي وضع من قبل
عدّة رجال بدو واستخدم هؤلاء الرجال القوة في نشر هذا الفكر
حيث كان الناس غير مخيرين: إمّا أن تعتنق الإسلام أو تقتل.

لقد توصلت الى قناعة أنه لا يوجد شيء إسمه الله فهو
بدعة من الناس، فلم أعد أؤمن بوجوده ولا بأي شيء سماوي أي
أصبحت ملحدا ، لذا إتجهت للعالم أحاول أن أمتع نفسي، صحيح
أنّي لم أكن مؤمنا بوجود الله ولكنّي في نفس الوقت لم استطع أن
أستمتع بحياتي فما زال شعوري بالحزن وفقدان السلام الداخلي
والضياع وعدم وجود أمل بحياة جيدة كانت كل هذه الهواجس
تتجثم على صدري، مما إنعكس سلبا على تصرفاتي مع الناس

المحيطة بي، أخوتي وأصدقائي، لقد أصبحت شخصا كئيبا جدا ومتشائما لدرجة فكرت أن أنتحر.

صحيح ان الفكرة قد تكون مخيفة ولكنها بالنسبة لي ليست كذلك فجميع الناس الذين حولي كانوا يعتقدون أنني إذا إنتحرت سأذهب للجحيم وكنت اضحك من افكارهم هذه، فأنا لم أكن مؤمنا بوجود الله في الأصل فكيف أؤمن بوجود الجحيم ؟! وهنا وفي ذلك الوقت إستخدم الله أصدقاءً لي وعائلتي وأقنعوني بالسفر إلى خارج العراق.

قد يكون لتغيير المكان وفرصة الحصول على وظيفة جديدة مع ثقافة جديدة قد يساعد ذلك على تغيير افكاري ونفسي الداخلية وأتوقف عن الأفكار السوداء وفعلا سافرت إلى إحدى دول الجوار وهي الدولة الوحيد في ذلك الوقت التي كان ممكن للعراقيين السفر إليها وصلت إلى تلك الدولة في شهر تموز سنة 1999 وكانت خطّة الله معدّة لي هناك.

العثور على طريق الله

عندما وصلت إلى تلك الدولة بدات أبحث عن وظيف تدريس في إحدى الجامعات فقد كنت أحمل شهادة عليا في العلو لكن بعد مرور ستة أشهر لم استطع الحصول على وظيفة، وبدات النقود لدي تنفذ فما كان منّي إلاّ أن أبحث عن أي عمل أستطي منه تسديد إحتياجاتي وفعلا وجدت عملا في شركة في وسد المدينة وكان صاحب الشركة لديه مكتبة خاصة فيها الكثير مر الكتب التي كان ممنوع تداولها في الدول الإسلامية وهذه الكتب تتحدث عن كيفية بناء الإسلام ومن اين جاءت فكرة الإسلا وكيف أن محمد تزوج بنت عم القس ورقة بن نوفل راعي كنيس قرب مكة في ذلك الوقت وكيف أن هذه الطائفة كانت مطرودة مر قبل روما لأنهم لم يكونوا يؤمنوا ان المسيح هو الله ولكنهم كانو يؤمنون أنه نبي ورسول من الله ولديه معجزات كثيرة، وهذه هي الفكرة التي نقلها محمد في القرآن وغيرها من قصص الأنبيا والتاريخ اليهودي، وايضا كانت هذه الكتب تتناول لماذا بدأ الإسلا كدين في مكة يحترم الديانات الأخرى ويؤمن بحرية الفكر وا

إكراه في الدين، لكن بعدما إنتقل إلى يثرب او " المدينة المنورة لاحقا" وأصبح قوّةً عسكريةً تغير إلى دين قمعي ودكتاتوري، وأحل قتل كل من يعارضه .

بعد إطلاعي على هذه المعلومات والتي أسقطت القشور من عيوني بدأ لسان حالي يسأل أنه على مر السنين لم يكن لدي أي سلام مع الدين الإسلامي لأنه فعلا ليس دين من الله هذا يقودني في المقابل الى الاعتراف ، ان الله قد يكون فعلا له وجود لكن أين وكيف أستطيع ان أجده؟ هنا في هذه اللحظة تذكرت الشخص المسيحي الذي كان يدرس معي في الجامعة ولم تسنح لي الفرصة في ذلك الوقت لأتحدث معه تذكرت أنه كان شخصا يتمتع بحياته الجميلة و هو لطيف جدا ، لذا فكرت أن أطّلع على القرآن المسيحي[5] الذي تربى ذلك الشخص عليه فبدأت ابحث عن كتب تتحدث عن المسيحية فقرأت ما تيسر في المكتبات وكان كلّه سلبي يتحدث عن الجانب السيء فقط عن التاريخ اليهودي والمسيحي ولكنّي لم أحب ذلك فقد كنت ابحث عن الديانة المسيحية وليس التاريخ حيث رحلتي هي في الأساس رحلة بحث عن الله لذا قررت

[5] لم أكن أعرف أنّه يدعى الكتاب المقدس

أن اذهب إلى مكتبة مسيحية وأشتري بعض الكتب المسيحية، وفعلا ذهبت إلى إحدى المكتبات وأشتريت بعض الكتيبات الصغيرة وبدات بقراءتها ولكنّي لم أكن أفهم بعض الكلمات مثلا ماذا تعني الروح القدس؟ ماذا يعني الله واحد موجود في ثلاثة اقانيم؟ واشياء أخرى لم استطع فهمها لأني قضيت جلّ حياتي أقرأ وأتعلم ثقافة وتاريخ إسلامي بلغة قرآنية لذا كان من الصعب أن افهم هذه المصطلحات المسيحية لذا فكرت في طلب مساعدة من شخص كان يتعامل مع الشركة التي كنت أعمل فيها ، إذ كنت أعرف من خلال إسمه أنّه مسيحي، ولما إلتقيت به سألته بعض هذه الأسئلة ولكنه قال :لا توجد عندي أجوبة على هذه الأسئلة، ولكنّي يمكن ان تذهب للكنيسة وتسأل وهم سيجيبون على اسئلتك. وشجعني هذا الشخص وأقنعني بان أذهب للكنيسة بأسئلتي وفعلا بعد عدّة أيّام أخذت هذه الأسئلة وذهبت ابحث عن كنيسة ووجدت في وسط المدينة كنيسة كبيرة بأبراج عالية مع وجود صليب كبير أعلى البرج كنت اشعر بالرهبة لحظة دخولي باحة الكنيسة فاستقبلني في الطريق شخص يلبس جلبابا اسود مع قبعة سوداء وكان يضع الصليب على عنقة وكان ملتحيا أيضا ، فعندما رأيته تصورت أنّه إمام الكنيسة قدّمت له نفسي إسمي محمد

الحلاّج هذه خلفيتي وأنا الآن أقف هنا ابحث عن الله فهل لك ان تشرح لي ماذا يعني الله لك؟ وكيف تتصور الله في مخيلتك هل هو جبّار منتقم؟ ام هل هو رحيم لطيف؟.

أكملت طرح سؤالي عليه وكنت انتظر الإجابة ولكن الإجابة كانت غير ما توقعت فقد تحدث هذا الرجل وطلب منّي الخروج من الكنيسة وسألني بلطف أن لا أعود مرّة أخرى!! ماذا؟؟؟ ... ماذا يعني هذا الجواب؟ لم أستطع أن أتحدث بأي شيء حينها ولكنّي غادرت خجلا منزعجا واشعر بغضبٍ شديد، فقد تعلمت منذ نعومة أظافري أن لا أناقش الإمام فلم أنبس بأي حرف مع إمام الكنيسة، ولكنّي ذهبت لذلك الشخص الذي قال لي أن أذهب للكنيسة وصببت عليه ثورة غضبي ومع كل الكلام النابي الذي قلته لهذا الشخص إلاّ أنّه كان فقط ينظر لي ويرسم على وجهه إبتسامة خفيفة أمتص بها غضبي فقال بعد أن هدأت ثورتي أن هذا الكاهن لم يستقبلك لأنه يمكن أن يكون خائفا منك حيث تصور أنّك تعمل مع المخابرات، لذا كان هذا ردّه ،لكن في الجانب الآخر أن الله كانت له يد في الموضوع وسألته باستغراب ماذا تعني بذلك؟ فقال لي أن هذه الكنيسة طقسية جداً لذا فبحثك

عن الله في هذا المكان لن يفيدك كثيرا لأنهم مثل الإسلام الذي كنت تشتكي منه يوجد الكثير الكثير من القدّيسين الذين تحولوا من خدّام المسيح إلى اشخاص تعظمهم الناس وتطلب منهم ونسوا قول المسيح "كل ما تطلبونه باسمي تأخذونه" فأعطى الناس هؤلاء القديسين مكان الله.

الخبر الجيد من قبل هذا الشخص هو أنّه وعد بأخذي إلى كنيسة أجد فيها الله وفعلا دلّني على كنيسة (...) الإنجيلية وكانت المرة الأولى التي أدخل فيها كنيسة في شهر نيسان سنة 2000 حيث المرة الأولى ارى فيها الكنيسة من الداخل وأستمعت إلى الموسيقى وكانت جميلة جدا مع كلمات ترانيم جميلة ايضا فاستمتعت جدا بالتسبيح، لكن الشيء الغريب الذي حصل في ذلك اليوم أن القسيس عندما بدأ يتكلم كان كلامه موجها لي فقط أو هذا ما شعرت به فقد كنت افكر في قرارة نفسي كيف عرف القسيس أنّي أزور الكنيسة للمرة الأولى وكيف عرف أني أبحث عن الله ففكرت في داخلي ممكن أن الشخص الذي دلّني على الكنيسة يمكن ان يكون قد أتصل مع القسيس وأخبره عنّي، لكن في الحقيقة بعد فترة علمت أن هذا الشيء لم يحصل فقد كانت

الرسالة في ذلك اليوم هو كلام خاص من الله لي فقد إستخدم الله القسيس ليتكلم معي من خلاله.

بعد نهاية الإجتماع إقتربت من راعي الكنيسة وقدمت له نفسي إسمي محمد الحلاّج وهذه خلفيتي وهذا ما أؤمن به وأنا الآن أبحث عن الله من خلال ديانتك! إنهيت تقديمي وأنتظرت ان يطلب منّي الخروج وعدم العودة مرة ثانية أو هذا ما كنت أتوقعه لكن الخبر السار كان في جوابه "أهلا وسهلا هذا بيت الله وهو مفتوح للجميع فأهلا وسهلا بك في اي وقت" وأعطاني الكتاب المقدس وكانت هذه هي المرة الأولى التي ألمس فيها الكتاب المقدس حيث في الإسلام كان محرماً علينا أن نقرأ أو حتى نلمس الكتاب المقدس وأنتابني شعور غريب لحظة مسكت الكتاب المقدس بين يدي شعور غريب جداً فقد شعرت برعشة خفيفة في الجسد وشعرت بسلام في النفس هذه كانت لحظاتي الأولى في الكنيسة، ومنها بدات أسلك في طريق الله.

بداياتي مع المسيح

في الأيام الأولى لسلوكي في طريق الله عانيت من حروب شديدة من عدو الخير "إبليس" والذي حاول ان يثنيني عن طريق الحق، وحينها لم أكن أعلم أن هذه الحرب من إبليس حيث إعتقدت أن الله غاضب منّي لأني تركت الإسلام وأحاول الدخول إلى المسيحية، لكنّي لم استسلم وواصلت السير في طريق الله.

بدأت منذ الليلة الأولى التي صار فيها عندي كتاب مقدس أقرأ بنهم كل ليلة حيث كان يوم عملي طويل يمتد إلى إحدى عشرة ساعة ولكنّي كنت في كل يوم أذهب للكنيسة بعد نهاية عملي حيث كنت أذهب إلى كنيستي يوم الأحد في الإجتماع العام والإثنين كان هناك خدمة خاصّة للعراقيين ويوم الأربعاء درس كتاب مقدس أمّا الثلاثاء فقد كانت هناك خدمة في كنيسة (...) الأنجيلية كنت احضرها وكان عندهم درس كتاب مقدس يوم الخميس أما يوم الجمعة فكان عطلة اسبوعية كنت اذهب صباحا إلى الكنيسة الأفريقية ومساءً إلى إجتماع آخر ويوم السبت كان

هناك درس كتاب مقدس مع مجموعة بيتية وكل مساء عندما أعود للمنزل كنت آخذ معي الكتاب المقدس إلى الفراش وكنت أقرأ تحت "البطانية" خوفا من زملائي في السكن أن يروا معي الكتاب المقدس حيث كنت اسكن مع شخصين مسلمين، لكن رغم التعب الجسدي بسبب طول يوم عملي إلاّ أنّي كنت أستمتع جداّ بقراءة الكتاب المقدس خصوصا ومع مرور الوقت إكتشفت أن أكثر من ثمانين بالمئة من الشريعة الإسلامية مأخوذة من الكتاب المقدس " وخصوصا من العهد القديم " .

بقيت على هذا الحال لفترة إمتدت من شهر نيسان سنة 2000 ولغاية شهر تشرين الثاني سنة 2001، خلال كل هذه الفترة لم أكن مؤمنا بأن المسيح هو الله وهو حي ومازال يعمل على خلاص النفوس. لم أكن مؤمنا أن هذا هو الطريق المؤدي الى السماء برغم ذلك وبرغم عدم إيماني الصريح لكنّي بقيت مستمراً بالذهاب كل يوم للكنيسة لأني كنت أشعر بسلام داخلي للمرة الأولى بحياتي ولأني كنت احب القراءة في الكتاب المقدس وايضا كان الناس في الكنيسة لطيفين جداّ معي، والجدير بالذكر هنا أن الناس داخل الكنيسة لم يكونوا يعرفوا أنّي مسلم فانا طلبت

من القسيس أن لا يعرف أحدٌ بذلك فأنا أعيش في بلد إسلامي وكنت أخاف من المسلمين أن يعرفوا بذلك وهذا قد يسبب لي ممكن بدون قصد مشاكل أنا في غنى عنها وكنت أواظب على الذهاب للكنيسة كل يوم وكان الله يعمل بداخلي من دون أن أعلم .

الولادة الروحية

كنت في يوم من ذلك الشهر أعاني من مشكلة صحية فقد كنت أعاني من ألم شديد في الجانب الأيمن من بطني وايضا تعب في كل جسدي، وهذا شيء طبيعي بسبب الجهد الكبير في العمل الطويل والذهاب مساءً الى الكنيسة، كل هذا سبب لجسدي العناء والتعب ، وفي ذلك المساء عندما إنتهى راعي الكنيسة من رسالته سأل إن كان أحد يحتاج إلى صلاة خاصة ممكن أن يتقدم للأمام فكنت أول الواقفين لأني كنت فعلا محتاج إلى صلاة خاصة بسبب حالتي الصحيّة وقفت في الأمام مع بعض الأشخاص الآخرين رفعت يديّ للأعلى وأغمضت عينيّ وبدات أتكلم مع الله وشعرت أن يداً وضعت على كتفي لكن اللمسة كانت مختلفة فبمجرد أن لمستْ هذه الكف كتفي أختفى الألم الذي كنت اشعر به في بطني وبدات اشعر ان جسدي بدأ يتغير مثل تمثال حجري يتحول إلى جسد بشري، فكل التعب والمرض في جسدي بدأ يزول، وشعرت ببرودة تسري في جسدي وتعرّقت وكان هناك شعور بالإنتعاش ، شعور رائع جدّا وبعد أن شعرت أن جسدي اصبح جديدا، بدأت

اشعر أيضا أن فكري بدأ يتغير وبدات الأفكار السوداوية التشاؤمية تخرج منه.

كنت أشعر أن هناك عملية تطهير لعقلي من كل الأفكار التي ممكن أن توصف بأنها شيطانية حتى شعرت بأني منتعش روحيا وافكار صافية تدخل عقلي وكياني ، ولأول مرة في حياتي لم أكن اشعر بضغط نفسي، وكان لدي سلام رائع جداً وفجأة شعرت ان هناك يداً إنتزعت قلبي ووضعت قلبا جديدا محله يفيض بالسلام والمحبة بشعور لم أختبره قبل ذلك وأستمرت هذه العملية قرابة العشر دقائق بعدها شعرت أن التعب يسري في يدي الممدودتان للأعلى وفي رجلي أيضاً! واستغربت من راعي الكنيسة حينها وتساءلت لماذا بقي القسيس يصلي معي كل هذه الفترة وترك الناس الباقين ينتظرون؟ .

لقد كنت أريد إنزال يدي فلم أستطع الإنتظار أكثر ففتحت عيني لأرى ما الذي دفع الراعي للبقاء معي كل هذه الفترة في الصلاة ولكنّي حين فتحت عيني لم أجد أحداً قربي فقد كان القسيس بعيداً في الجهة الأخرى من الكنيسة ولم يكن أحد من الأخوة بقربي، علمت أنه رب المجد يسوع المسيح هو الذي

لمسني واعطاني جسدا جديدا وفكرا جديدا وقلبا جديدا وحياة جديدة أيضا.

بعد تلك الليلة أختلفت حياتي جذرياً فلم اعد ذلك الشخص الضائع دون هدف في الحياة ودون أمل، كنت أصحو كل صباح وفكري وقلبي يفيضان فرحا وسلاما، حتى الناس من حولي والّذين كنت أتعامل معهم كل يوم شعروا بقوة التغيير التي حصلت فيَّ، ولمسوا قوة السلام التي تفيض بداخلي، وأيضاً قراءتي للكتاب المقدس أصبحت مختلفة، فقد كنت اقرأ الكتاب المقدس قبل هذه الليلة ككتاب تاريخي أو قصّة لكن بعد تلك الليلة صارت قوة الروح القدس تعمل بداخلي فصرت أقرأ الكتاب المقدس بالروح فأرى ما لم أكن أراه من قبل، قبلَ تلك الليلة كانت من أصعب الأمور التي كنت أعاني من صعوبة في فهمها، ألا و هي مسألة الثالوث لكن بعد تلك الليلة كنت استغرب من نفسي لماذا لم أكن أفهم شيئا بسيطا مثل ذلك؟؟ وصارت لدي شجاعة بأن أخبر بعض الأشخاص ولأول مرة من خارج الكنيسة عن إيماني وماذا حصل لي ولكنّي كنت حذراً في نفس الوقت فلم تكن لدي الشجاعة لأواجه الكل بإيماني الذي يمكن أن يوصف بايمان الأطفال وصرت أنمو في الإيمان والكلمة بالشركة الدائمة من خلال الصلاة

بالتحدث مع الله وأيضا مع الأخوة في الشركة الروحية ودراسة الكتاب المقدس.

أبو عبد الله وصوت المسيح

كان عملي يتطلب منّي في بعض الأحيان المرور بوسط المدينة ومن خلال ذلك كنت أرى دائما شخصا مشرّدا يسكن على الرصيف ولكنّي لم افكر يوماً أن أتكلم معه خوفاً من رد فعل غير محبب، لكن في إحدى المرات كنت أمرّ على مكتبة في وسط المدينة وكان هذا الشخص المشرد يجلس على زاوية الرصيف وعندما نظرت إليه جاء صوت من داخلي إليّ قائلاً إذهب وكلمه عن الله! في اللحظة التي سمعت الصوت فيها لم أكن متأكدا أنه صوت الله فماذا يريد الله من شخص مشرّد لا عقل له وكيف سيفهم هذا الشخص محبة وفداء المسيح، وفعلت مثلما فعل يونان تركت المأمورية وحاولت أن أهرب إلى الجهة المقابلة لكن صوت الله جاء ثانية وبصورة أوضح من المرة الأولى "أذهب وقل له أن المسيح يحبك" أمام هذا الأمر لم يكن لدي خيار لذا عدّت أدراجي ولكن كيف أوضح لهذا الشخص المشرد محبة المسيح رأيت على الزاوية الأخرى من الشارع محل لبيع الحلويات فذهبت واشتريت بعض الحلويات وضعتها في صحن وأقتربت بحذر من هذا الشخص

المشرد وجلست على الرصيف مقابله وكان ينظر لي بأستغراب فقدمت له صحن الحلويات وقلت له "هذا من المسيح عيسى بن مريم وهو يحبك" فأخذ الصحن منّى ومسك الملعقة ورماها على الأرض وبدأ يأكل بيده وهو يدمدم "نعم وأنا.. وأنا ..أحبه أيضا" نظرت حولي وفكرت ماذا يمكن أن أقول أكثر فلم أجد شيء لذا وقفت وبدأت بالإبتعاد عن هذا الشخص وفجأة مسك بيدي شخص كان يقف بقرب هذا الشخص المشرد وكان يراقبني ويستمع لي حينما أقتربت من هذا الشخص المشردوسالني الشخص الثاني قائلاً

"هل أنت مسيحي؟"

في البداية ترددت وسألته بدوري :

"ذلك يعتمد إذا كنت من المخابرات فأنا مسلم وإذا لم تكن من المخابرات فأنا مسيحي"

فضحك ورد قائلاً:

"لا تخف فلست أعمل في الدولة لكن لدي سؤال لك؟"

فقلت: " سلّ"

فقال": في كل يوم نسبكم ونشتمكم انتم المسيحيين ونجعل إلهكم مجرد نبي يأتي بعد نبينا وحقوقكم مسلوبة في عدّة دول إسلامية ولكنكم لا تتحركون ساكنا، في المقابل ماذا نفعل نحن المسلمين بعد نشر صور النبي محمد في جريدة في اوروبا؟ التي كلّما هرب مسلم من إضطهاد إحتضنته أوروبا أقول بعد نشر هذه الصور قمنا نحن المسلمين في عدّة دول بمظاهرات وحرقنا سفارات ولو تمكنّا من قتلكم لما ترددنا فلماذا تقابلون أنتم المسيحيين كل هذا الإضطهاد بالسكوت لماذا لا تتحركون وتثورون على الظلم"

وبصراحة أعجبني السؤال فقلت له: "**لا تنتقموا لانفسكم ايها الاحباء بل اعطوا مكانا للغضب.لانه مكتوب لي النقمة انا اجازي يقول الرب**"(رومية 12:19) وايضا يقول الرب "**أحبّوا أعدائكم**" وعندما قلت هذه الكلمة الأخيرة صعق الرجل فكيف تستطيع أن تحب عدوّك؟ كيف تحب من يؤذيك ويهينك ويكرهك؟ هذا شيء غريب لكنّي حاولت أن اشرح له أن هذا الأمر ليس إختيارا لنا إذا أردنا أن نحبهم أم لا، فوصية المسيح واضحة هنا أن نحبهم يعني محبة الأعداء واجبة وأيضاً يجب أن نصلي لهم، والرب يأمرنا بذلك وهو يعرف أننا لن نستطيع فعل ذلك بمفردنا وبدون مساعدته لنا لذلك يجب أن نطلب منه

المساعدة حتى نكون على صورته ونحياة حياة مسيحية، لم يسعفني الوقت في التحدث كثيرا فكان لا بدّ ان أعود لعملي فأعتذرت منه لكنه كان يحب أن يستمع للمزيد فقلت له أن ينتظرني بنفس المكان الساعة الثامنة ،أي بعد إنتهاء عملي وفعلا في نهاية اليوم لمّا جئت وجدته ينتظر فذهبنا سوية إلى منزلي وتحدثنا حتى الساعة الحادية عشرة مساء وكان سعيدا جدا بما يسمع وطلب نسخة من الكتاب المقدس ليقرأ فيها وطلبت منه ان اصلي له فلم يمانع فصليت وأعطاني الرب هذه الكلمات الخاصة له:

"أيها الرب يسوع رب المجد قد يكون سهلا علّي أن أتصرف بصورة جيّدة امام الناس ولكّن يا رب انت فاحص القلوب وتعرف ما بداخل قلب الإنسان لأنه من القلب ينبع الخير والشر ولن أستطيع أن أخفي عنك شيء ساعدني يا رب أن أتغير على تلك الصورة التي رسمتها بحياتك على الأرض حياة خالية من المعصية وملآنة بالطاعة والمحبة، أعلم أنّي لن استطيع ذلك لوحدي لكن يا رب ارجوك ساعدني واعطني قوّة لأسلك في طريق المحبة

واستثمر حياتي بالشهادة للناس عن محبتكَ ، لك كل المجد للأبد آمين " .

وجاء وقت الإنصراف وكان مرتاحا جداً فمشيت معه حتى الباب وبدون شعور مددت يدي وأعطيته بطاقتي الخاصه فأنا في العادة أكتب إسمي على ورقة مع رقم التلفون في حال أن الشخص لديه اي سؤال أو يحب أن يسمع أكثر عن المسيح لكن هذه المرة وبحركة لا إرادية أعطيته بطاقة العمل وكان الإسم المكتوب عليها هو محمد الحلاّج فلما نظر إلى الإسم سألني باستغراب عمن يكون محمد الحلاج ؟فقلت

"أنا إسمي محمد الحلاّج"

فتعجب من ذلك وقال

"كيف مسيحي ومبشر بالمسيح وأسمك محمد لكنه صمت وقال تصبح على خير" وذهب لكن بعد ذهابة بفترة قصيرة عاد جرس الباب ليرن مرة ثانية ولما فتحت كان هو الشخص نفسه ابو عبد الله فقال

"لو كنت مسيحي وتتحدث عن المسيح وكم هو جميل هذا شيء عادي كنت ساذهب للبيت فرح بما سمعت منك لكن

الأمـر هنا مختلف فأنـت مـسلم فلماذا تتحـدث كـذلك ما الـذي حصل لك؟"

وهذا أكثر سؤال أحبة ما الذي حصل لحياتك؟ فقلت اهلا وسهلا بك مرة ثانية وتحدثنا حتى الساعة الثانية بعد منتصف الليل وقبل المسيح كمخلص شخصي له وذهب بسلام، بعد هذه الليلة بحوالي عشرة أيام إتصل بي ابو عبد الله وقال أنه يريد ان يودعني فهو سيعود إلى بلده فاستغربت وسالته اين يكون بلدك فذكر لي أنه من السعودية وجاء الى هذه البلاد لأن أبنته تحتاج إلى عملية في القلب ولقد تمت عمليتها بنجاح وسنعود بها إلى البلاد ولم اسمع من ابو عبد الله شيء بعد ذلك لكن تأملوا معي طرق الله العجيبة فهـو إستخدم مـرض إبنته ليأتي بـه إلى هـذه الدولـة واسـتخدم شخصا مشردا ينام على الرصيف كنت أراه طيلة الخمس سنوات السابقة لهذا اليوم ولم أفكر بالإقتراب منه لكن الله إستخدم هذا الشخص المشرد حتى يسمع ابو عبد الله الرسالة واستخدم ايضا إسم "محمد" ليثير تساؤلات داخله ويعود ويسأل ماذا حصل لحياتك وفي النهاية سلم حياته للرب يسوع رب المجد وذهب وأنا اثق أن كل شخص لديه خطّة خاصة لحياته من رب المجد لكن

هل تحب أن ترى فعلا عمل رب المجد في حياتك؟ إسأل أخي الحبيب وأختي الغالية ورب المجد يقول كل من يسأل يأخذ لكن إسالوا بإيمان إطلبوا من رب المجد أن يريكم الطريق الصحيح أنا هنا لا أطلب منكم تغيير ديانة أو أي شيء من ذلك.. لا يا أخوتي الأحباء فالمسلم ليبقى مسلم والسيخي ليبقى سيخي واليهودي ليبقى يهودي وأي شخص يسلك بأي ديانه هي يعرفها فليبقى كما هو لكن ليجلس مع نفسه ومع الرب وليتحدث إليه كصديق أو كأب او أي صفة أنت تريدها تحدث معه وأطلب منه أن يظهر مجده في حياتك وصدقني أنا أتحدث عن حياة أعيشها كل يوم بل كل لحظة عندما يظهر مجد الرب يسوع في حياتك ستعرف معنى آخر للسلام والمحبة ولن تستطيع إلاّ ان تحب وتحب وتحب وتصور معي طعم الحياة عندما تعيشها في محبة سأصلي لك الآن ويمكن أنت أن تصلي هذه الصلاة بعدي وأنا أثق أن الله يسمع صلاتك..

اشكرك يا رب لأنك تحب جميع الخطاة وأوهم أنا ..أشكرك يا رب لأنك الراعي الصالح لنا أشكرك يا رب لأنك تعتني بنا وتهتم بكل صغيرة بحياتنا ساعدني يارب أن أتحرر من الخطيئة

ساعدنى لأرى مجدك والمس وأتذوق سلامك في حياتي شكرا لك يارب لأنك غفرت خطاياي ساعدني ان أتخلص من سطوة العالم على نفسي وأن أعيش لك وأن أقدم محبتك لمن يسيؤون إلّيّ أثق يارب انك تسمعني لك كل المجد آمين.

إشتداد الحرب

أعطاني الرب نعمة أن أكوب السبب في أفراح معدّة في السماء حسب كلمته في لو 15:10 "**هكذا اقول لكم يكون فرح قدام ملائكة الله بخاطئ واحد يتوب**" وقد إستخدم الله فترة إعداد طويلة لمّا كنت في البرية ابحث عن الله في كتب الإسلام والقرآن ولأن الله كلّي المعرفة فقد إستفدت من هذه الفترة، بعد أن ابصرت النور ومن خلال المعلومات التي اكتسبتها من القراءة المتنوعة في الكتب الاسلامية والمسيحية، صار سهلاً عليّ أن أتحدث مع الأحبة المسلمين من خلال القرآن والكتب الأخرى عن المسيح، وفعلا ربحت بعض النفوس الضالة إلى ملكوت الله، ولكن هذه الثمار أزعجت عدو الخير إبليس لذلك إستخدم جنوده لكي يعطل الخدمة، فلقد جلست في إحدى المرات مع شخص من خلفية مسلمة شيعيه وكنت أشاركه رسالة المحبة وكيف كانت حياتي قبل لقائي برب المجد وكيف هي حياتي معه ملآنه بالسلام والفرح وأبلغته رسالة الخلاص لكن هذا الشخص كان يستمع إلى في الظاهر لكن من الداخل كان يفور غضبا منّي وبعد عدة ايام عاد

هذا الشخص إلى العراق وهناك ذهب إلى مجموعة تسمى جيش المهدي[6] وهذا الجيش تشكل من مجموعة شباب متهورة وجاهلة يقودهم شخص جاهل بالدين كان أبوه رجل دين كبير وهذه هي الطريقة الإسلامية فالحكم وراثي لذا بعد أن مات رجل الدين تسلم إبنه المنصب وهو لا يفقه شيئا، فشكّل مع هؤلاء الشباب عصابات لقطع الطرق والقتل والإرهاب وكان لهم نفوذ كبير بعدّة دول في الشرق الأوسط منها الدولة التي أقيم فيها، لذا بعد أن علموا عنّي من قبل ذلك الشخص إتّصلوا بي هاتفياً أول الأمر وهدّدوني وذكروا لي كل المعلومات عن مكان الكنيسة التي أذهب إليها والناس الّذين ألتقي بهم وأعطوني فرصة لمدّة إسبوعين لأعلن توبتي وأعود إلى الإسلام، في واقع الأمر لم اتفاجأ في البداية فأنا أعلم أنني أعيش في بلد مسلم وأعمل في وسط مسلم وأيضاً إسمي محمد وبكوني أذهب للكنيسة واعتنق المسيحية كأسلوب حياة لي كل هذه الأشياء اضعها بالحسبان انه في يوم ما سأتعرض للمضايقة وأسمع كلاما غير محبب سماعه. لذا بعد أن أنهوا المكالمة أغلقت الهاتف وعدّت

[6] وهو حركة مسلحة شيعية متطرفة تتبع في تعليماتها للتيار الصدري بقيادة رجل الدين الشيعي مقتدى الصدر ، وبالإمكان البحث أكثر عن هذه الحركة في الإنترنت إذا رغبتم بالحصول عن معلومات أكثر عنهم

إلي العمل ولكن بعد ذلك بثلاثة اسابيع من تاريخ هذه المكالمة جاء ثلاثة اشخاص إلى مكان عملي يسألون عنّي وعندما دخلوا إلى المكتب حيث كنت أجلس قدموا نفسهم على أنّهم من نفس المجموعة التي إتصلت بي وكانوا يراقبون تحركاتي.

وأنا ما زلت اذهب للكنيسة وأبشر الناس بالمسيح لذا آثروا أن يعطوني إنذاراً أكثر جديّة من المرة الأولى بان يأتوا بأنفسهم لمكان عملي وبصراحة هذه المرة خفت قليلاً فوجود ثلاثة اشخاص في مكتبي لا يبعث على الطمأنينة بالبتة لذا حاولت أن أمتص حقدهم وكراهيتهم التي كانوا يحاولون ان يوضحوها لي كمرتد عن الاسلام وحاولت أن أنهي الحديث بسرعة فذهبوا بعد أن توعدوني بتنفيذ القصاص الشرعي إذا إستمريت على كفري وضلالي وقالوا : أنّهم يراقبون كل تحركاتي ويعرفون كل شيء عنّي اين أذهب وبمن التقي، ولأكون صريحا فقد شعرت هذه المرة فعلاً بالخوف منهم، فهؤلاء أناس اشرار وايضا كان خوفي على بعض الأخوة المؤمنين من الخلفيات غير المسيحية الذين أقوم بزيارتهم خفت أن يفعلوا شيئا سيئا مع هذه العائلات، شاركت راعي كنيستي وبعض الأصدقاء بذلك فتوقفت عن زيارة بعض

الأصدقاء خوفاً وحرصاً عليهم من هذه المجموعة الإرهابية، ولكنّي في نفس الوقت كنت مواظبا على الذهاب للكنيسة، فانا لا أستطيع أن أبتعد كثيراً عن شركة المؤمنين.

وبعد مرور شهر تقريباً على زيارة هؤلاء الأشخاص لي في مكتبي، وكان يوم أنهيت عملي فيه مساءً وذهبت إلى البيت وحوالي الساعة التاسعة مساءً رن جرس الباب إستغربت في البداية فأنا لم أكن أنتظر أحداً فلم يتصل بي أحد مثلاً ليطلب زيارتي ولكنّي فكّرت ممكن أن يكون المؤجّر صاحب البيت أو أحد الجيران فقمت وفتحت الباب ووجدت رجل على الباب يسألني "هل أنت السيد محمد الحلاّج؟" أجبته بنعم، وسأل ثانية "هل ممكن أن آخذ من وقتك دقيقتين لنتحدث؟" وكان من الصعب أن تقول لا لأنه كان يتحدث بلطف إضافة لثقافتنا العربية التي توجب علينا دعوة الزائر للدخول فطلبت منه الدخول ولكن حصل شيئا فاجأني، فلقد كان معه أربعة اشخاص كانوا يقفون على الزاوية البعيدة بحيث لم يتسنّ لي رؤيتهم ولما طلبت من الشخص الدخول تفاجأت بهم جميعا داخل بيتي فاستغربت وطلبت منهم الخروج، لكن قائد المجموعة تكلم وقال نحن نريد ان

نتحدث معك فقط وبصراحة فلم يكن أمامي خيار آخر سوى الإستماع إليهم وطلبت منهم الجلوس ورفضوا دعوتي لهم أن يشربوا اي شيء وبدأ قائد المجموعة بالتكلّم وقال:

"نحن إتّصلنا بك على تلفونك الخلوي وأرسلنا لك اشخاصا إلى مكتبك.."

وهنا عرفت من هم هؤلاء المجموعة إنّهم من جيش المهدي، فقلت نعم صحيح حصل ذلك وإستمر قائد المجموعة بالحديث وأعطيناك فرصة للتوبة والرجوع عن كفرك وإرتدادك والعودة إلى حضن الإسلام ولكنّك لم تستمع إلينا لذا فقد إجتمعت المحكمة الشرعية في الجامعة العلمية الشيعية في العراق وقرروا تنفيذ القصاص الشرعي بك واخرج ورقة من جيبه وقرأ عليّ نص الحكم والذي يتكون من بعض الآيات من القرآن وأكيد تلك التي تتحدث عن قطع الرقاب، ودعّم حديثة ببعض الأحاديث لنبي الاسلام محمد وبعض رجال الدين الشيعة والتي توضح أنّه في حال أصرّاري على كفري وضلالي يجب أن ينفذ عليّ الحد وهو "قطع الراس" وأعطوني خياراً واحداً وهو أن أعلن توبتي أمامهم وأعلن الشهادات الثلاثة (كونهم شيعة فالسنة لديهم شهادتين فقط) وأقيم معهم الصلاة لطلب المغفرة من الله وإلا فأن ذنبك في رقبتك،

وهنا بدأت حديثي وقلت لهم أنا لا أعترض عمّا قلتم فهذا ما ترونه أنتم ما فيه مرضاة الله ولكنّكم عندما دخلتم قلتم نريد أن نتحدث فلنتحدث الآن إسالوني لماذا تركت الإسلام؟ لماذا إخترت المسيح لأتبعه؟ ماذا وجدت مع المسيح ولم أجده في الإسلام؟إسالوني هذه الأسئلة ولنتحدث عن المسيح من خلال القرآن[7] الذي تؤمنون انتم به ولكنّهم في واقع الحال لم يأتوا ليسمعوا فقد خافوا من المناقشة لذا رفض قائدهم النقاش وقال انّهم جاؤا لتنفيذ قرار ولم يأتوا للنقاش فحاولت معهم كثيراً لكنّهم فعلاً لم يأتوا ليسمعوا بل ليقتلوني، وبعد أن تعبت معهم وجدت انّه لا يوجد أمل لدي بالحديث معهم فحاولت الهرب من الشقّة لكن مع وجود خمسة رجال حولي ومتحفزين للقتل كان من الصعب الهروب فأمسكوا بي وطرحوني أرضاً فسقطت مرمياً على ظهري فوقف شخصان منهم على ركبتيَّ وقيدوا رجلي وأثنان منهم وقفوا على ذراعي وقيّدوهما فلم أستطع الحركة وكنت أشعر بأن ركبتي سوف تنكسر من ثقل الرجل الذي وقف عليها، امّا قائد المجموعة فكان بيده

[7] فمن خلال دراستي لفترة طويلة للقرآن أكتشفت أن في القرآن تعتبر أعظم شخصية مذكور عنها هي المسيح وكان يمكن أن أشرح لهم ومن خلال القرآن أن المسيح هو روح الله وكلمته وهذا ما أؤمن به أنا

سكين فوضع حذائه على راسي ليحفظ إتجاه وجهي إلى الكعبة فالطريقة الإسلامية لقتل دجاجة أو خروف يجب أن يكون وجهة الضحية بإتجاه الكعبة وفي اللحظة التي وضع فيها رجله على رأسي مرت أمامي حياتي على شكل فيلم فكانت صور سريعة من طفولتي والإعدادية وعائلتي وسفري إلى خارج العراق والكنيسة وأخيراً صرخت "اين انت يا رب؟" ، كنت ممدداً على الأرض ووجهي بموازاة السجّادة وفجأة تحول وجه السجّادة إلى وجه بحيرة متلألئ وظهر رب المجد يمشي على هذا الماء بوجهه الجميل وبابتسامته العذبة في اللحظة التي رأيت فيها وجهه لم اعد اشعر باي الم بجسدي والرعب الذي كنت اشعر فيه بصدري تحول إلى نوع من السلام لم آلفه من قبل رغم مرور سبع سنوات مع المسيح وقتها وبالرغم من انّي اعيش بسلام ونعمة في كل لحظة معه لكن نوع السلام الذي شعرت به عندما رأيته وجه لوجه.

كان سلاما من نوع مختلف، قلت في اللحظة التي رأيته فيها لم أعد اشعر بأي الم بجسدي فكان تخيلي للوهلة الأولى انهم قطعوا راسي وأنا الآن مع المسيح في السماء ولكنّه تحدث وقال "لا تخف فلن يستطيعوا أن يفعلوا اي شيء لك!" وهنا شعرت أنّي ما زلت في العالم ولكنّي صرخت وطلبت منه أن يأخذني معه فلا اريد

ان ابقى في العالم بعد ان تذوقت طعم السلام في محضره وقلت "لا يارب أرجوك خذني معك، لا أريد العودة للعالم" وكنت أنتظر السكين أن تنزل على رقبتي لكنّهم تأخروا! لماذا لم يذبحوني؟ فلمّا فتحت عينيّ وجدتهم قد تركوني ووقفوا بعيداً عني وكانت وجوههم خائفة وكانّهم شاهدوا شيئاً أخافهم فلم استطع النطق بأي شيء وكنت ما زلت ممدداً على الأرض أنظر بدهشةٍ لهؤلاء الرجال ماذا حصل لهم؟ فتكلم قائدهم بصوت مرتجف وقال سنعطيك فرصة لمدّة إسبوعين يجب أن تغادر فيهما هذه البلاد.. وخرجوا مسرعين فماذا حصل لهم ما الذي رأوه وجعلهم يتركوني بهذه الصورة؟

كان الموقف اشبه بحلم أو رؤيا لكنّي لّما أستجمعت قوتي كنت ما زلت على الأرض وبشعورين غريبين الأول كان شعور بالفرح لأني ما زلت حيّا، والشعور الثاني كان الحزن فقد أنتهى وقت اللقاء القصير مع المسيح وجها لوجه، تشددت وتشجعت وقمت لأستوعب ما حصل وفهمت قول الرب حينها" لأنه من يمسكم يمس حدقة عينه. زك 2:8" وفعلا كان إختبارا عمليا ومعجزيا لعناية الرب باولاده.

بعد هذه الليلة اصبح عدو الخير إبليس لديه مشكلة كبيرة معي.. فبعد إختبار عناية الله الفائقة، صرت لا أخاف من العالم وتولدت بداخلي جرأة أكثر في مشاركة الناس رسالة المحبة والخلاص، ولكن بعد مرور عدّة اسابيع وبعد أن فشل إبليس في إستخدام جنوده من جيش المهدي لأرجاعي عن طريق الحق كان هناك جوله أخرى مع جنود من نوع آخر هذه المرة.

الفرح الكبير

قد يكون بعض الناس وأنا منهم سمعنا عن المخابرات في العالم الثالث وخصوصا في العالم العربي وكيف يعاملون البشر وكيف إذا دخل شخص في غياهب ودهاليز المخابرات فهناك أمل قليل بأن نراه مرّة أخرى، كنت قد أستقليت سيارة أجرة من مكان سكني إلى مكان عملي في إحدى الصباحات وتكلمت مع سائق سيارة الأجرة عن عمل الله بحياتي وكيف خلّصني من مخالب الموت وكان لدي نسخة بيدي من الإنجيل أعطيتها له كهدية وعندما وصلت إلى مكان عملي أعطيته بطاقتي في حال لديه أي أسئلة وعندما نظر إلى البطاقة نظر إلى إسمي وقال "كيف هذا مرسل ومبشر بالمسيح وأسمك محمد الحلاّج؟ كيف هذا وأنت مسلم؟" فشرحت له أن المسيح هو للكل وأول الناس نحن المسلمين الذين نحتاج المسيح فعلاً في حياتنا فالمسيح قال الاصحاء لا يحتاجون إلى طبيب بل المرضى هم من يحتاجون إلى طبيب لذا فنحن نحتاج إليه أكثر من غيرنا، وكان سائق سيارة الأجرة هذا حسب ما حصل بعد ذلك يعمل مع جهاز المخابرات في تلك البلاد

فلم يمر إلاّ يوم واحد حتى كان رجال المخابرات لدي في الشركة في اليوم الثاني فاخذوني إلى السجن ووضعوني في غرفة صغيرة في اللحظة الأولى التي أغلقوا فيها الباب صار عدو الخير يعرض امامي صور التعذيب وكيف سيقتلعون اظافرك وكيف سيطفئون السجائر على ظهرك وكيف وكيف وجميع الصور التي نعرفها عن تعامل المخابرات مع المسجونين تحت الأرض لكنّي حتى أكسر عمل إبليس بدأت ارنم قد تكون الكلمات الأولى من الترنيم كانت تخرج بصوت مرتعش لكن بعد بضع كلمات شعرت بقوة غريبة وبفرح عظيم فارتفع صوتي في الترنيم لدرجة إنزعج منها الضابط فصرخ فيّ أن أصمت ولكني لم أصمت فاستمريت في الترنيم ولم أكن اعرف من اين جائني السلام والفرح فجأة في مكان مثل ذلك المكان ولكنّي علمت فيما بعد انّه في تلك اللحظات كان هناك الكثير من المؤمنين يرفعوني بالصلاة وكانت مشاعر السلام والفرح تلك هي ثمرة صلاتهم وهذا ما يذكره الكتاب ان نصلي لبعضنا البعض، بقيت في السجن لمدة خمسة أيام كان التحقيق إستمر في اليوم الأول لمدة ثمانية ساعات كان يتحدث معي الضابط وكأنه يريد ان يفترسني ولكنّي لم اشعر بالخوف ابداً وكان الموضوع بالنسبة لي مجرد تسلية وبعد خمسة ايام في السجن لم يجدوا شيء يفعلوه مع هذا

المجنون بحب المسيح غير ان يبعد إلى العراق وأصر الضابط أن ابعد براً إلى العراق مع أنّي طلبت منه السماح لي بالسفر جواً وعلى حسابي الشخصي لكنّه رفض فقد كانت الطريق البرية مغلقة من قبل القاعدة في ذلك الوقت من حدود ذلك البلد حتى بغداد ولذلك كان يخطط لأعدامي من قبل رجال القاعدة والذي يحملون رسالة موت إلى العالم فأهم يفرح بالموت لذا وضعوني في سيّارة حمل وبعد مسيرة تسع ساعات وصلنا الحدود التي تفصل تلك البلاد عن العراق وبعد ان أخذوا بصمات الأصابع والعيون ووضعوا الختم الأحمر على جواز سفري اشاروا إلى جهة الشرق وقالوا العراق من هنا أذهب.

ملائكة تستخدم سيارات الهمر

كان الوقت مساءً لا أعرف كم الوقت بالضبط حينما بدأت المشي بإتجاه العراق وبعد مرور ساعة ونصف تقريبا وصلت أول نقطة للجنود العراقيين فرحبوا بي بإستغراب لماذا امشي في الليل في هذه المنطقة الخطرة الملآنة بالعقارب والأفاعي والضباع وبصراحة لمّا اخبروني بذلك شعرت بمجازفة المسير في هذه المنطقة ولكنّي لم استغرب السلام الذي كنت اشعر به حين قطعت تلك المسافة وبدون أيّة مشاكل فانا متأكد أن الله كان معي يحميني كعادته وبقيت على الحدود لمدة يومين تقريبا أصلي إلى الله أن يريني الطريق لأذهب إلى عائلتي فلقد كان هناك طريقان: الأول يمر عبر مدينة الفلوجة وحينها كانت مقراً للقاعدة فلم يكن من الممكن أن أنفذ من هذا الطريق والطريق الآخر هو أن أنحدر جنوبا واعود إلى أهلي ولكن هذه الطريق كانت تمر من مناطق جيش المهدي، وهم الذين حاولوا قتلي قبل فترة لذلك جلست اصلي واطلب من رب المجد أن يريني مشيئته لماذا يارب سمحت أن اخرج من هذا المدينة فالأكيد أن أحداً لا يستطيع أن يخرجني

بدون موافقتك فما هي مشيئتك يا رب؟ بعد مرور يومين تقريباً على جلوسي على الحدود جاء شخصان إليّ وسألاني هل أود الذهاب معهم إلى دمشق عاصمة سوريا؟ وأستغربت ذلك فأنا أصلي طالباً من الله أن يريني طريقاً أسلكه في التوجه لأهلي في العراق فهل مشيئته الذهاب الى سوريا؟

طلبت من هؤلاء الأشخاص خمس دقائق. أخذت مكانا منفردا وركعت على ركبتيّ وصلّيت وسألت الله عن مشيئته في ذلك فهل مشيئته هي كذلك فقال الله لي "قم إذهب"، وهنا بدأت مشكلة أخرى وهي كان يجب أن نجد سيارة تقلّنا من الحدود حيث أنا جالس إلى الحدود العراقية السورية، وبعد فترة إنتظار وجدنا سيّارة يمكن أن تقلّنا ولكن السائق قال أننا سنسير مسافة 150 كيلوا مترا تقريبا شرقاً بإتجاه الفلوجة وبعدها مسافة 170 كيلوا مترا تقريبا شمال غرب بإتجاه الحدود السورية وجميع هذه المناطق التي سنمر بها توجد عناصر للقاعدة وفي حال أمسكوا بكم سيقطعون رؤوسكم[8] وهنا قلت للسائق لا تخف فهذه مشكلته هو

[8] مثلما يعرف الجميع فإن رسالة القاعدة للعالم هي القتل وكوننا لم نكن معهم من ضمن المذهب الوهابي التكفيري فهذا سبب يعتبر كافي بالنسبة لهم لقتلنا

وليست مشكلتنا !! وهنا نظر إلّي السائق بأستغراب وقال: مشكلة من تقصد؟

أجبته أنها مشكلة الله فهو الذي قال لي ان أذهب،لذا فحياتنا بين يديه والحفاظ عليها هي من ضمن مراحمه علينا، لذا توكل على الله وتحرك فنظر إلى السائق نظرة فهمت منها أنّه ظنّ اني مجنون.. وفعلاً تحرّك السائق من الحدود.

الآن حاولوا أن تتصورا معي الذي حصل، بعد إنطلاقنا من الحدود وبمسافة لا تتجاوز الألف متر وكنّا نسير على الطريق السريع ظهرت فجأة على الجانب الأيمن لنا ثلاث سيارات من نوع همر والتي يستخدمها الجيش الأمريكي في العراق وكانت هذه السيارات محملة بالجنود الّذين يتسلحون بمدافع رشاشة وكانت المسافة بيننا حوالي مئة متر، وكانوا يسيرون بموازاتنا وكان ظهورهم فجأة ودون سابق علامة! فالكل يعرف أنّه عندما تقود سيارتك على الطريق الدولي السريع فعندما تقترب منك سيارة أخرى تبدأ بنقطة بعيدة وتقترب منك رويداً ومع الأقتراب يزداد حجمها تدريجيا هذا ما يقوله المنطق، لكن ما حدث هنا أنّهم ظهروا فجأة، ناهيك أننا كنّا نسير في منطقة صحراوية، فتعجب كل الراكبين معي! فمن أين جاء هؤلاء الجنود؟ ظهور هذه

السيارات بجانبنا أشعرني بالإطمئنان بأننا في حفظ من القاعدة ولو إلى حين.

إستمرت سيارات الهمر تسير بجانبنا بإتجاه الشرق حتى بلوغنا التقاطع الذي نغير إتجاهنا فيه بإتجاه الحدود السورية والمعجزة كانت أنهم غيّروا إتجاههم معنا وقبل بلوغنا الحدود السورية بمسافة إختفت هذه السيارات بصورة مفاجئة حتى أننا لم نستطع أن نرى اي غبار في الجو أو أي اثر لهم! وصار الشخص الذي يجلس بجانبي يشد شعره ويصرخ ما هذا؟ اين ذهب هؤلاء ماذا يعني ذلك؟ أمّا انا فكنت أبتسم لأنّي اعرف أنهم ليسوا بجنود بشرية بل ملائكة ارسلهم الله ليحموا إبنه، واشعرني فعلاً أنني خاص في عينيه.

وصلنا الحدود السورية وهنا نظر الشخص الذي كان معي ورأى في جواز سفري الختم الأحمر من المخابرات في تلك البلاد وقال بإنزعاج : كان يجب أن تقول لنا ونحن على الحدود أنك لديك مشاكل مع المخابرات هناك؟ وهنا إستغربت قوله ولماذا كان يجب أن يعرف هناك، وما الفرق؟ قال أن البلدان العربية مختلفة دائما فيما بينها لكنها متفقة من ناحية التعاون المخابراتي فيما

بينهم، لذا كون لديك مشكلة مع المخابرات في أحد البلدان هذا يسبب لك المشاكل مع معظم دول الشرق الأوسط، ويكون إسمك على اللائحة السوداء، وهنا قلت له أنها ليست مشكلتي وأنما مشكلة الله فحين صلّيت وسالته قال: إذهب، لذا هو يعرف كيف يسيّر الأمور، فضحك هذا الشخص من إيماني فدخلنا سويّة على المكتب وكان هناك أربعة رجال شرطة يستلمون جوازات السفر فتقدمنا لأول شبّاك فأعطى الشخص الأول جوازه مصحوبا بخمسين دولار أميركي، "كان على جميع العراقيين دفع هذا المبلغ للحصول على تأشيرة الدخول". فأخذ الشخص الأول جوازة مع تاشيرة زيارة لمدّة إسبوعين، تقدّم الشخص الثاني وكان نفس الترتيب جواز السفر مع خمسين دولار أميركي وتأشيرة زيارة لمدّة إسبوعين، وهنا جاء دوري تقدّمت وأعطيته جواز سفري وكنت أضع في جيبي ورقة نقدية من فئة مائة دولار أميركي لأعطيها للشرطي في حال طلبه المال، إذ كنت أتوقع أن ينظر الختم الأحمر ويقول لي آسف لا نحب الأشخاص الذّين يعملون مشاكل أو توقعت أن يرسلني للضابط، لكن الذي حدث كان شيئا لم أتصوره، فبعد أن مسك الشرطي جواز سفري بيده بدأ يتحدث مع الشرطي الآخر الذي يجلس بجانبه ففتح جواز

سفري ولم ينظر إلى صورتي كما هي العادة على الحدود ليتأكدوا أنه جواز السفر الخاص بالمسافر ولم ينظر حتّى إلى صلاحية أو تاريخ نفاذ جواز السفر بل فتح على صفحة خالية من الأختام ووضع التاشيرة في تلك الصفحة وكتب تأشيرة زيارة لمدّة شهر!! لم تصدّق عيناي ما ترى، فالمسافران اللّذان سبقاني دفعا مبلغا من المال وحصلا على تاشيرة زيارة لمدّة إسبوعين وأنا لم أدفع شيئا وحصلت على تأشيرة زيارة لمدّة شهر!! كم هو عظيم إلهنا .. دخلت إلى سوريا وعشت أياما رائعة جداً أتم الله كلمته لي حينها، ولكن ماهي كلمة الله لي والتي قلت الآن أنّه أتمها في سوريا؟ إليكم الحكاية..

كلمة الله

كنّا في المدينة التي إلتقيت فيها المسيح نجتمع كل ليلة راس سنّة في كنيسة (...) الإنجيلية نصلّي إلى الله ليبارك السنة الجديدة ويعطينا أن نربح نفوساً جديدة له وكان في ليلة رأس السنة عام 2007 أن الله تكلم معي ووعد ببركات كثيرة لحياتي سأستمتع بها خلال سنّة 2007 فأنا في تلك البلاد كنت ولمدّة ثمان لم استطع خلالها أن أزور أهلي في العراق أو أن يأتوا هم لرؤيتي، فقد منعت الحكومة في تلك البلاد إعطاء تاشيرة دخول للعراقيين إلا من كان منهم في الحكومة البعثية السابقة والذين كانوا يأتون إليها محملين بثروات العراق أو من معه رصيد يفوق المليون دولار أميركي يضعه في البنوك ومعظم هؤلاء كانوا ممن سرقوا البنوك في العراق حين دخول القوات الأمريكية للعراق وبما أن عائلتي لم تكن تتمتع بهذين الشرطين لذا لم يستطيعوا أن يأتوا لزيارتي، وأيضاً كان من الصعب أن أكوّن عائلة في تلك البلاد فلم أستطع الزواج من بنت مسيحية مؤمنة كون جميع أوراقي الثبوتية تدل على أنّي مسلم لذا ففي حال زواجي يكون جميع أطفالي حسب القانون مسلمين

ولم أجد وسيلة لحل هذه المشكلة فلم يكن هناك أي شخص مسيحي يريد أن يكون أحفاده مسلمين لذا كان الخيار هذا صعب وايضاً في حال أنّي وجدت بنت مسلمة تتفهم حالتي وتقبل الزواج منّي كان أهلها سيرفضون كوني مسلم مرتد عن الإسلام، لذا لم يكن هناك لدي اي تخطيط للزواج وتكوين عائلة.

وهذا ما جعلني أفكر بماذا سيبارك الله حياتي خلال سنة 2007 ويجب ان لا تنحصر أفكاري ببعض الأمور الدنيوية، لكن ما الذي حصل بعد ذلك وكيف كانت بركات الله لحياتي فقد حاولت مجموعة من جيش المهدي قتلي وايضاً دخلت السجن وطردت من تلك الدولة إلى سوريا" كما ذكرت في الصفحات السابقة" وطبعا بعد طردي من تلك الدولة لم أحمل معي سوى بعض الملابس فقد تركت كل شيء خلفي هناك وأنا في حيرة من أمري أفكر ما الذي حصل وأين هي بركة الله لحياتي التي وعدني بها وقال أنّه سيباركني في سنة 2007 وفعلا كان وعد الله أمين فلقد فتح الله باب البركات على مصراعيه بعد دخولي إلى سوريا فبعد ثمانية سنوات لم أرى أهلي فيها كان سهلا أن نلتقي في سوريا فأجتمعت مع أهلي هناك وبعد أن قررت أن أعيش حياة عزوبية

لمجد المسيح أعطاني الله زوجة لم أكن أتخيل في افضل أحلامي ان يكون لي زوجة أفضل وأجمل وأروع منها وهي التي قال سليمان عنها "**ثمنها يفوق اللآلئ**" وبعد أن كانت خدمتي في البلد الذ ي إلتقيت فيه بالمسيح مقيّدة بسبب عدم تفرغي الكامل للخدمة لحاجتي للعمل هناك، فتح الله باب للخدمة الواسعة في سوريا فالشعب السوري شعب منفتح ومتفهم للأديان وكون الشعب السوري هو أكثر الشعوب إنفتاحاً وحيث دمشق من أكثر المدن إحتضاناً للتنوع الديني في دول الشرق الأوسط لما لديها من تاريخ مع المسيحية جعلها مفتوحة أكثر لعمل ولبركات الله واستخدم الله الوقت الصعب في العراق ليأتي العراقيين إلى سوريا ويكون مجال الحصاد في وسطهم مثمراً جداً وأعطانا الله بركة في عيون الناس هناك وربحنا بعض النفوس البعيدة عن الرب وأدخلناهم إلى ملكوته واصبحوا خدّام للمسيح هناك، وبالحق يجب أن أقول أنّني أعيش حياة تعكس الآية التي تقول "**ما لم تر عين ولم تسمع أذن ولم يخطر على بال إنسان ما أعّده الله للذين يحبونه**" 1كو 2:9 فكانت حياتي فعلا **أروع من حلم** أعيشه مع الله في كل يوم ففي كل لحظة أفكر فيها أو ألقي نظرة فقط على حياتي الماضية قبل المسيح كنت استغرب كيف بقيت حيّا طوال تلك السنين بدون

المسيح لكن مع المسيح الحياة لها شكل آخر يمكن أن يوصف بأنها **أروع من حلم**.

هنا أكتفي بما أريد مشاركتكم به عمّا عمل الله في حياتي فالحياة مع الله تجد فيها كل يوم بركة خاصة وأختبار خاص تتذوق فيه محبة المسيح، ولكنّي لن أتركم تذهبون قبل أن أحدّثكم عن صورة أخرى عن قدرة عمل الله فالصورة التي رسمها الله لحياتي قد بدأت بالبحث عن الله وبعدها وجدته بأن أعلن نفسه لي ولكن توجد صور أخرى عن الله وهي صورة حيّة أخرى، عدي محمد فهو صورة أخرى لقوة عمل الله؟

إختبار عدي محمد

عدي محمد

إلتقيت بعدي وكان شخصا مؤمنا بالمسيح فقد إفتقده الله من مرضة الذي أفقده بصره وأعاد له المسيح بصره فكيف حدث ذلك؟ لكم الحكاية بصورة مختصرة.

لأني أريد أن أعطي فرصة لهذا الشخص بعد أن يخرج من الشرق الأوسط أن يحدثكم بنفسه عن قصّته مع المسيح وايضاً لا أريد أن أذكر الكثير من التفاصيل عنه لأنه ما زال حتى لحظة كتابة هذه الكلمات يخدم الرب يسوع في الشرق الأوسط فما هي حكايته ؟

ولد عدي في عائلة مسلمة تدين بالمذهب السنّي في جنوب العراق،وهي عائلة كبيرة نشأ وترعرع على الإسلام وكان لديه عمل خاص به منذ صغره وقد يكون بسبب الحروب الكثيرة والتي كانت مدينة البصرة حيث ولد عدي مسرحا لها سبب رئيسي أنّه لم يكمل دراسته ،فبعد خدمة الجيش ذهب ليبدأ مشروعه الخاص وتزوج بعدها من بنت الجيران والتي كانت من خلفية شيعية وباركهم الله باربعة أطفال ولغاية هنا فالحياة طبيعية فعدي لديه

عمله الخاص وبيته وعائلته وكل شيء يسير جيدا لغاية سنه 2002 حيث عانى عدي من مرض في الرأس ولم تكن العناية الطبية في العراق في ذلك الوقت تسمح بعلاجه بسبب ظروف الحصار الإقتصادي والحروب الكثيرة التي عانى منها العراق فكان نتيجه ذلك أن عدي فقد نعمة البصر وتحول من رجل صاحب عمل وعائلة وحياة مستقرة إلى رجل ضرير وطبعا فأن زوجته لم تتركه وتجلس وإنّما حاولت وفي كل الإتجاهات أن تساعد زوجها وأخذته لعدة أطباء وكل طبيب أجرى عملية جراحية في مكان مختلف ولكن بعد مرور تقريبا سنه وبعد أربعة عمليات جراحية كانت النتيجة أن عدي تحول إلى رجل ضرير وقد باع كل ما يملكه لاجراء العمليات الجراحية والعلاج وأنتقل للسكن مع عائلته حيث أعطوه غرفة واحده يسكن فيها هو وزوجته الحامل مع اربعة أطفال وكانت أياما صعبة جدّا على عدي فهو بعد الذي حصل له كان يفكر أن ينتحر حتّى يخفف عن زوجته الحمل ويرتاح هو ايضاً من العذاب الذي كان يشعر به فالحياة صعبة جداّ بدون بصر وخاصة مع وجود عائلة كبيرة تقع تحت مسؤوليته.

اللقاء مع المسيح

في ذلك الوقت الصعب كان يحتاج عدي لأي امل لشفائة لذلك عندما ذكر له الناس عن طبيب في بغداد العاصمة يمكن أن يساعده لم يتردد فسافر بمعية زوجته إلى هناك وألتقوا مع الطبيب وكان المستشفى الذي يديره هذا الطبيب مزدحما جداً، وكان موعد العملية بعد شهرين لكن مع توسلات عدي ودموع زوجته وخصوصية الحالة أعطاهم الطبيب موعداً بعد ثلاثة أيّام لأجراء العملية الجراحية لعينية مع نسبة نجاح قد تصل إلى 40٪ لكن بالنسبة إلى عدي فهذه نسبه عالية فلم يكن لديه شيء يخسره، كانت الثلاثة أيام قبل موعد العملية الجراحية غير كافية للعودة للمنزل في الجنوب والعودة مجددا لأجراء العملية الجراحية، لذا قرروا أن يسكنوا هذه الأيام في غرفة في أحد الفنادق القريبة من المستشفى وفي أول ليلة طلب عدي من زوجته أن تصلي وتتضرع لجميع الأنبياء التي تعرفهم من القرآن أن يتدخلوا وتكون هذه أخر عملية جراحية له، فبدأت الزوجة تصلي وتدعوا الله بشفاعة الأنبياء الذين تعرفهم وكان عدي ينصت لها وقلبه يصلّي حتى

وصلت زوجته إلى النبي عيسى بن مريم فلمّا بدأت تصلي بأسم المسيح عيسى بن مريم غطّ عدي في نوم عميق فقد كان آخر شيء سمعه هو أسم المسيح عيسى بن مريم ولمّا رأت الزوجه أن عدي غطّ في النوم ذهبت هي بدورها للنوم وفي تمام الساعة الثالثة من فجر ذلك اليوم كان عدي ممددا على ظهره في الفراش وفجأة أنشق الجدار المقابل له في غرفة الفندق ودخل شعاع من نور ملأ الغرفة وبدأ ظل رجل يلوح لعدي لكنّه لم يستطع أن يتبين وجهه لشدّة النور المشع منه فصرخ عدي من أنت؟ فأجاب الرجل لا تخف جئت لأخلّصك واشفيك، فصرخ عدي ثانيةً من أنت؟ فأجاب الرجل مرة ثانية لا تخف فقد جئت لأخلّصك واشفيك ولمّا وصل هذا الرجل إلى مكان عدي حيث كان ممدداً في سريره أحتضن الرجل عدي وهنا شعر عدي بسلام عجيب كان قد إفتقده من زمن طويل وتمنى أن يبقى هذا الرجل يحتضنه إلى الأبد فوضع الرجل راس عدي على الوسادة ولمس عيني عدي بإبهاميه وذهب ولمّا خرج بدأ عدي يصرخ لا تتركني إبقى معي ارجوك لا تتركني ارجوك وهنا إستيقضت زوجته على صراخه وتصورت أن لديه كابوس بسبب حالته الصحية والنفسية وحاولت أن تهدأه وتصور له أن هذه المرة ستكون العملية الجراحية ناجحة

ويستعيد بصرة لكن المفاجأة السارّة حصلت هنا أن عدي كان يبصر في هذه اللحظة وقال لزوجته لن أحتاج العملية الجراحية فأنا الآن إبصر ففكرت الزوجة للوهلة الأولى أن زوجها فقد عقله مع بصره وأصبح مجنوناً ولكنّه بدأ يذكر لها لون الستائر في الغرفة ولون السجادة وحتى لون شراشف السرير وهنا أغمي على الزوجه وسقطت على الأرض من المفاجأة وبعدما صحت أخبرها عدي بالرؤية التي حصلت معه وهنا تذكرت الزوجة وقالت أنّها عندما صحت من النوم على صراخه رأت نور يدخل في الحائط لكنها فكرت إنها تحلم بسبب إستيقاظها من النوم فجأة فلم تفكر في ذلك النور.

في اليوم التالي عاد عدي وزوجته إلى البصرة وأستقبلهم الأهل بالفرح وعبارات المديح لهذا الطبيب الماهر الذي شفا عدي بسرعة كبيرة فقد ظنّ الأهل أنّه أجرى عملية جراحية لكنه أخبرهم بما حصل معه وكيف أن شخص ما زاره ولمس عينيه وشفاهما وقال أنّة المخلص والشافي لي ولكنّي لم أستطع أن أتبين من هو.

الطريق المؤدي كرب وضيق

بعد ان أخبر عدي عائلته بالرؤيا وكيف أن ذلك الرجل قد لمس عينيه وشفاهما هللت عائلته وقالوا أنّه النبي محمد حيث أهله من السنّة ولكن عائلة زوجته فكانوا شيعة قالوا لا هذا الذي شفاه هو الإمام علي!!

وبدأ كل شخص يمدح معتقده ويضفي عليه صفة معجزة شفاء عدي، ولكن عدي لم يكن يشعر ولا يثق بأي من هؤلاء الذين يذكروهم فهو قد أفنى حياته في إسترضائهم والتبرك بهم ولم يكن لهم أي دور في حياته وخصوصا في مرضه فلم يتحرك اي ميت منهم للشفاعة أمام الله لكن هذا الشخص الذي شفاني قال أنّه جاء ليخلصني ويشفيني فمن هو المخلّص والشافي وهنا بدأت الضغوط تزداد على عدي من أهله وأهل زوجته وايضاً من الحركات الإسلامية المدعومة من قبل ايران والقاعدة أيضا والمدعومة من قبل السعودية والتي نشطت بعد سقوط نظام صدام ودخول الجيش الأمريكي للعراق كلّ ذلك شكل ضغطاً نفسياً على عدى وصار يفكّر ويبحث عن هذا الشخص الذي أعطاه حياة جديدة فقد كان يريد ان يقول له شكراً ..ولكن من هو؟

دخل عدي في دوامة صراع نفسي اثر كثيرا عليه حتى أنّه في إحدى المرات تمنّى لو أنّه لم يشفى فجلس في غرفته وتكلم مع هذا الشخص وقال له أرجوك إظهر مرة ثانية وقل لي من أنت؟ بعد هذه الليلة بعدّة ايام وبينما كان عدي يسير في الشارع إلتقى باحد الأصدقاء وكان شخص من خلفية مسيحية فبارك هذا الرجل المسيحي لعدي الشفاء قائلا:مبروك سمعت أن محمداً قد شفاك! لكن عدي أجاب أن الذي شفاني ليس محمداً؟ وهنا تفاجأ الرجل المسيحي من جواب عدي فالكل كان خائفاً من الحركات الإسلامية فكان يجب أن يقول محمدا شفاني حتى يحفظ نفسه، فسأله الرجل ثانية ومن تعتقد أنّه شفاك؟ فقال عدي لا أعرف لكنه قال لي أنّه يخلصني ويشفيني فمن هم المخلص والشافي؟ فقال الرجل لعدي إذهب للكنيسة وأطلب منهم الكتاب المقدس وأقرأ في الإنجيل وستعرف من هو المخلّص، لكن عدّي رفض ذلك قائلا أنه مسلم ولن يستطيع أن يلمس الكتاب المقدس فهذا حرام فتركه هذا الرجل هنا وذهب في طريقه فعاد عدي مساءً وجلس يفكر في كلام الرجل ولأنّه يريد ان يعرف من الذي أعطاه حياة جديدة ذهب بعد ثلاثة أيّام إلى كنيسة في وسط المدينة وهناك تكلّم مع سيدة تعمل في الكنيسة وطلب منها الكتاب المقدس، في البداية

ترددت السيدة فقد كانت مثلها مثل مئات الآلاف من المسيحيين في العراق الّذين تعرّضوا للأضطهاد خلال تلك الفترة لكن مشيئة الله تدخلت هنا حيث كانت تلك السيدة قد سمعت عن قصة عدي لذا وافقت أن تعطيه الكتاب المقدس لكن ليس بيده فقد وضعته على الأرض ودخلت إلى الداخل وطلبت من عدي اخذ الكتاب المقدس بعد دخولها إحترازا منها فيما لو مسكوا عدي معه كتاب مقدس فستنكر هي أنّها أعطته الكتاب فهي قد وضعته في الخارج وهو أخذه، أخذ عدي الكتاب المقدس وذهب إلى البيت وهناك جلس مع زوجته يقرآن في إنجيل لوقا وقبل إنتصاف الليل عرف عدي من هو الّذي شفاه وخلّصة لذا فما كان منه إلاّ أن مسك الكتاب المقدس بيده وأخذ يقفز من الفرح في وسط البيت وهو ينادي على أمّه وإخوته،، يريد أن يشاركهم فرحه لكن المفاجأة كانت قاسية عليه فحين جاء اخوته إليه وجدوا الكتاب المقدس بيده يرفعه عالياً وهو يصرخ المسيح المسيح هو الذّي شفاني فبدلا من أن يشاركوه في فرحه إنهالوا عليه ضربا وإتهموه بالإرتداد وأرادوا قتله فطرحوه مع عائلته في الشارع فأخذ زوجته وأطفاله وهرب خارج المدينة حيث سكن على المنطقة الحدودية بين العراق والكويت حيث كانت منطقة محرمة على القوات العسكرية

دخولها بعد ان حاول جيش المهدي وحزب ثأر الله وايضا مجموعات أخرى قتله وكان يقتات مع أطفاله من القمامة .

وفي وسط هذه الصعاب مات الجنين في بطن زوجته والتي كانت حاملاً في شهرها السادس، وفي إحدى المرات التي نزل فيها إلى المدينة ليحضر لأطفاله بعض الطعام أمسكوه مجموعة من جنود حزب ثأر الله وأخذوه إلى مكان بعيد يريدون قتله فربطوا يديه إلى الخلف ووضعوا بعض الرصاصات في المسدس بغرض إطلاق النار على راسة لكن حدثت معجزة هنا حيث رأي الشيخ المقيم في ذلك المكان أن سعر الرصاصة دولار ونصف وهذا سعر غالي لكي يدفعوه في قتل شخص مرتد مثل عدي لذا طلب من الجنود إستخدام المثقاب في قتله بعمل ثقب في رأسه وهي طريقة مجانيةّ لذا أحضروا المثقاب وبدأ عدي يشعر بالهواء الناتج من دوران المثقاب على وجهه وفي هذه اللحظة رأي نفس صورة المسيح التي رآها اول مرة حين لمس عينيه وشفاها وهنا توقف المثقاب عن الدوران فقد إنقطعت الكهرباء وذهب أحد الجنود ليشغل مولد الكهرباء لكن لم يكن هناك وقود فارسلوا أحدهم ليحضر وقود للمولد الكهربائي وفي اثناء ذلك حضر لنفس المكان إمام من أئمة

الشيعة فسألهم عن قصة عدي فأخبروه بها فقال لهم لماذا تقتلونه الآن ارسلوا لأهله وليفتدوه بمبلغ من المال وأطلقوه وعودوا مرة ثانية وأقبضوا عليه وأيضا سيدفع أهله بعض المال ليفتدوه وهكذا يمكن أن تحصلوا من خلاله على المال، فأرسلوا أحدهم إلى عائلته ليطلب فديه منهم لكن أخوته قالوا لهذا الشخص إقتلوه نحن لا نريده فقد جلب لنا العار وفي اثناء هذه المحاورة كان أحد اصدقاء عدي حاضراً فقال أنا أدفع لكم أطلقوا سراحه وفعلاً دفع لهم مبلغ أربعمائة دولار أمريكي فأطلقوا سراحه وهنا قال هذا الصديق لعدي أنّهم سيقبضون عليه ثانية وفي النهاية سيقتلونه لذا حاول ان تهرب من العراق وقام هذا الصديق بمساعدة عدي في إستخراج جوازات سفر له ولعائلته وسافروا إلى أحدى بلدان الجوار ومازال عدي يعيش حتى لحظة طباعة هذا الكلمات في الشرق الأوسط يستخدمه الرب مع الناس هناك فحياته مثال لصورة الكنيسة الأولى نصلي إلى الله أن يستخدمنا أيضاً لأنتشار ملكوته.